The Complete
Idiot's Guide® to
Easy Artisan Bread

The Complete Idiot's Guide® to Easy Artisan Bread

by Yvonne Ruperti

ALPHA

A member of Penguin Group (USA) Inc.

ALPHA BOOKS

Published by the Penguin Group

Penguin Group (USA) Inc., 375 Hudson Street, New York, New York 10014, USA

Penguin Group (Canada), 90 Eglinton Avenue East, Suite 700, Toronto, Ontario M4P 2Y3, Canada (a division of Pearson Penguin Canada Inc.)

Penguin Books Ltd., 80 Strand, London WC2R 0RL, England

Penguin Ireland, 25 St. Stephen's Green, Dublin 2, Ireland (a division of Penguin Books Ltd.)

Penguin Group (Australia), 250 Camberwell Road, Camberwell, Victoria 3124, Australia (a division of Pearson Australia Group Pty. Ltd.)

Penguin Books India Pvt. Ltd., 11 Community Centre, Panchsheel Park, New Delhi—110 017, India

Penguin Group (NZ), 67 Apollo Drive, Rosedale, North Shore, Auckland 1311, New Zealand (a division of Pearson New Zealand Ltd.)

Penguin Books (South Africa) (Pty.) Ltd., 24 Sturdee Avenue, Rosebank, Johannesburg 2196, South Africa

Penguin Books Ltd., Registered Offices: 80 Strand, London WC2R 0RL, England

International Standard Book Number: 978-1-61564-004-1
Library of Congress Catalog Card Number: 2010920413

12 11 10   8 7 6 5 4 3 2 1

Interpretation of the printing code: The rightmost number of the first series of numbers is the year of the book's printing; the rightmost number of the second series of numbers is the number of the book's printing. For example, a printing code of 10-1 shows that the first printing occurred in 2010.

Printed in the United States of America

Note: This publication contains the opinions and ideas of its author. It is intended to provide helpful and informative material on the subject matter covered. It is sold with the understanding that the author and publisher are not engaged in rendering professional services in the book. If the reader requires personal assistance or advice, a competent professional should be consulted.

The author and publisher specifically disclaim any responsibility for any liability, loss, or risk, personal or otherwise, which is incurred as a consequence, directly or indirectly, of the use and application of any of the contents of this book.

Most Alpha books are available at special quantity discounts for bulk purchases for sales promotions, premiums, fund-raising, or educational use. Special books, or book excerpts, can also be created to fit specific needs.

For details, write: Special Markets, Alpha Books, 375 Hudson Street, New York, NY 10014.

Publisher: *Marie Butler-Knight*
Associate Publisher: *Mike Sanders*
Senior Managing Editor: *Billy Fields*
Senior Acquisitions Editor: *Paul Dinas*
Senior Development Editor: *Christy Wagner*
Senior Production Editor: *Megan Douglass*

Copy Editor: *Cate Schwenk*
Cover Designer: *William Thomas*
Book Designer: *William Thomas, Rebecca Batchelor*
Indexer: *Heather McNeill*
Layout: *Ayanna Lacey*
Proofreader: *Laura Caddell*

Contents

Appendixes

Introduction

Have you always been curious about how to bake a fresh loaf of bread but thought it was just too complicated and required too much skill—skill you didn't have? Have you ever wanted to bake healthful, homemade foods for your family but felt you just didn't have the time? If you're nodding your head "yes" right now, then artisan breads are for you!

When you make an artisan bread, you experience the process and satisfaction of making a bread with your own hands. The easy artisan breads in this book use a no-knead method that will change the way you think about food and baking. No heavy mixing, dough hooks, fancy bread machines, or even old-fashioned elbow grease allowed! Learn how this method has revolutionized and truly modernized from-scratch baking. With the no-knead method, the dough does most of the work for you, allowing you to easily fit healthful, freshly made bread into your hectic schedule. There's no doubt about it—no-knead hand-crafted breads are within the reach of today's cook.

To help eliminate the mystery and guesswork of from-scratch baking, I explain what's going on in that stretchy ball of dough from the moment you stir the ingredients together until you take your first bite of warm crusty bread. Easy-to-follow, step-by-step instructions seamlessly guide you to each perfect loaf. And the fun facts, historical tidbits, and kitchen tips I've sprinkled throughout are guaranteed to make baking fun!

Breads complete any meal, and these easy artisan bread recipes satisfy every bread lover's craving—from breakfast and sandwich breads to pizza and even dessert. Many recipes are even meals in themselves! Forget commercial mixes loaded with preservatives, or packaged breads that may have been sitting on a store shelf for weeks. These recipes are chock-full of healthful, fresh ingredients, and you can't get any fresher than breads coming from your own oven!

Even if you've never baked a loaf of bread in your life, these recipes will have you pulling bakery-style loaves from your oven like a pro. And once you've experienced the warm, comforting smell of freshly baked bread wafting out of your oven, you'll never want to make that extra trip to the bakery again!

A Recipe for Success

This book is organized into 4 parts and 15 chapters that contain recipes for all types of easy yeast and no-yeast breads.

Part 1, Bread Basics, includes an abridged history of bread and the important changes in bread-baking methods that have occurred throughout the years. I also explain the importance of using the right ingredients and the correct tools when making bread. Detailed descriptions and explanations are given for the techniques and methods used in every step of no-knead bread-making.

Part 2, Yeast Breads, dives into yeast breads, with emphasis on savory applications. Boules, long loaves, sandwich-style loaf pan loaves, and tiny breads are all covered here. Finally, we explore ancient flatbreads and meal-making pizzas.

Part 3, Breakfast and Holiday Breads, discusses the sweeter side of bread, including breakfast and holiday breads. Laminated breads are explained here, as are some of the more artful and technically challenging breads.

Part 4, Quick Breads, introduces the quick bread, a completely different type of bread that uses chemical leaveners rather than yeast. These are literally the "quickest" of all the no-knead breads. A cross between a cake and a bread, breads such as cornbread, soda bread, biscuits, and scones are all covered here.

In each of these parts, I've included a wealth of information to help you get started with artisan breads, including easy-to-understand explanations for how the easy no-knead bread-baking process works. Each recipe contains detailed instructions, and many helpful illustrations guide you along.

Three appendixes at the end of the book contain definitions to culinary terms and ingredients, and a resource list to help you locate baking ingredients and tools. I've also included a list of measure equivalents and common baking substitutions.

Some Things to Help You Out Along the Way

Each chapter also includes sidebars with kitchen tips, handy hints, and little tasty informative bites that will help you become a competent and educated baker. Here's what to look for:

LOAF LINGO

These boxes explain culinary terms to help increase your knowledge of baking.

BAKER'S DOZEN

These useful kitchen tips include shortcuts and substitutions, all to make the time you spend baking both efficient and enjoyable.

BREAD HEAD

These boxes contain recipe-related morsels and quirky culinary tidbits to inform and amuse you.

DOUGH DON'T

These expert suggestions guide you through potentially challenging situations in the kitchen, explaining what to specifically watch out for.

Acknowledgments

I'd like to thank my family for supporting me throughout my culinary career and for always requesting bundles of my baked treats. Thanks to my great grandmother, who instilled in me a love for baking, and to my mother, who showed me how homemade bread is worlds apart from anything store-bought. A special thanks goes to my roommate, Adelaide, who's patiently sacrificed our kitchen for this project, and who's never once complained about trying my bread "experiments."

Trademarks

All terms mentioned in this book that are known to be or are suspected of being trademarks or service marks have been appropriately capitalized. Alpha Books and Penguin Group (USA) Inc. cannot attest to the accuracy of this information. Use of a term in this book should not be regarded as affecting the validity of any trademark or service mark.

Bread Basics

From a basic French boule to a laminated croissant, baking bread ranges from the simple to the challenging. Regardless of the level of complexity, a few essential concepts and methods remain the same behind every baked loaf. Familiarizing yourself with these ensures that your breads come out perfect every time.

Successful baking begins with picking the right ingredients and knowing how to use them. Quality matters, and choosing the best ingredients propels you on your way to the yummiest result. Selecting the appropriate tools and pieces of equipment is also important. It makes the process of transforming raw ingredients to a baked loaf smooth and efficient and helps your outcome to be bakery perfect.

Most importantly—especially when doing no-knead baking—is to learn how to combine ingredients and handle your doughs. Proper mixing, resting, shaping, and baking all contribute to the success of your loaves. Understanding each step and why it's done takes the mystery out of bread-baking and makes it fun and enjoyable. The knowledge you learn in Part 1 puts the power to create beautiful and delicious artisan breads in your hands.

The Staff of Life

In This Chapter

- Man's relationship with bread
- The history of bread-making
- New bread-making machines and products
- At-home baking and the no-knead revolution

For most of us, bread is a part of everyday life. These days you can purchase bread just about everywhere, even at your corner gas station! It's almost impossible to imagine life without bread, yet most of us have probably never thought about where it all began, or how bread became such an integral part of our society.

The emergence and growth of bread follows the evolution of man and his inventions. In this chapter, we take a brief look at the history of bread and how it has evolved from a life-sustaining food to an easy, everyday luxury you can bake at home.

Bread for Sustenance

Long before early humans learned to make bread, seeds and grains were an essential part of their diet. To make the grains edible, they were cooked into porridges that crudely resembled the hot cereals we eat today (minus the flavorings and sugary toppings, of course). Early peoples learned that ground grains cooked faster, so primitive mortar and pestle tools were used to create the first flours.

As we began eating these boiled grains and flours, it's not a stretch to deduce that the first flatbreads evolved from these porridges. They were probably shaped and then cooked on hot surfaces.

The baking, or cooking, was a major accomplishment because it made the nutrient- and carbohydrate-rich flatbreads portable, and people could pack and carry them wherever they went, without any need for cooking. Think of them as our first convenience food!

Friendly Fermentation

Let's interrupt the history lesson with a few notes on the science of breads, starting with *fermentation*. Fermentation is the breaking down or decomposing of organic substances by bacteria and yeast. The end result of this process is alcohol and carbon dioxide gas. Bacteria and wild yeast are present all around us, and when they come into contact with moist foods such as grain cereals, fermentation begins.

As the wet dough sits, the yeast goes crazy, converting starches in the flour to sugar and giving off carbon dioxide gas that expands the dough. Also, complex reactions occur in the dough that produce compounds that both add flavor to the dough and relax the *gluten*. This gives the dough more stretch, enabling it to hold more gas.

LOAF LINGO

In dough, **fermentation** occurs when yeast converts sugars and starches into alcohol. **Gluten** is made up of the proteins glutenin and gliadin. When these proteins bind together in a dough, they create strong strands that are able to stretch, without breaking, as gases formed by yeast expand the dough.

The longer the dough is allowed to ferment, flavor continues to develop, gases continue to expand the dough, and compounds continue to soften the dough. However, the party only goes on for so long. The dough won't keep blowing up like a balloon. It will stretch as far as the gluten strands will allow. (The dough increases about double in size.)

Long fermentation is a process in bread-making when the baker extends the fermenting process under very specific conditions. Specifically, the dough is rested in a chilled state. Yeast have a favorite temperature they prefer to work in (between 90°F and 110°F). If the dough stays at this temperature, the yeast will ferment and expand the dough at a rapid rate. If the dough is kept cooler, it gives the dough time to fully soak up the water in the dough, before the yeast go nuts. The goal is to have a fully hydrated dough to reap the best results from the fermentation. Our no-knead doughs take advantage of long fermentations.

In the beginning, wild yeast in the air fermented cereal grains, and at first, humans enjoyed this in the form of beer. It took a little while, however, for us to make the leap from utilizing the fermenting abilities of yeast for beer, to bread. It's likely that while making primitive flatbreads, early people mixed beer with flour to moisten it, and began to recognize the amazing power of yeast.

The reason for all this is gluten. Gluten is a protein in wheat grains that forms long, stretchy strands when moistened. When the grain ferments from the yeast, the resulting gases cause the strands to stretch and expand, leavening these primitive doughs.

At the time, not all societies were using wheat grains. Many were using grains such as barley and oats—grains that didn't contain gluten and, therefore, the ability to stretch. So while pots of fermenting barley were bubbling over, the grains couldn't stretch and contain the expanding gases. These breads made from nongluten grains remained flat and dense. Societies that happened to be harvesting wheat grains were the lucky ones to discover the wonders of yeast leavening. They were the first to witness the rising powers of yeast in their buckets of fermenting grain mashes, and the first to witness the yeast as it expanded the dough again when cooked.

I can only imagine how magical and mysterious it must have been for early civilizations to see their doughs grow and increase in size right before their eyes!

The Earliest Bakers

As communities began to organize themselves into towns and cities, bakeries were created to bake for the masses. Both the flourmill and the bakery were usually located in the same spot, and people were trained and employed as professional craftsmen to make bread for the people of the city. Understanding the intricacies of fermentation and temperature for producing the best loaf was a valued craft. So much so, that bread craftsmen formed into special communal guilds to protect their livelihood and the art of bread-making. It was common for families to send a young teen to apprentice with a baker for years to learn the ropes.

BREAD HEAD

The earliest cookbooks didn't record recipes for bread because those recipes were protected by special bread guilds.

The conditions of early bakeries were most likely very poor. Large stone and clay ovens made for an extremely hot work environment, plus the bakeries were crowded with workers. And although bread-making was a craft, the pay was most likely pretty low. Because the loaves fed the masses, making it a volume business, prices and, in turn, pay were kept low.

Leavening on the Rise

Ingredients and methods for bread-making remained essentially the same until the end of the nineteenth century. Then with the beginning of the industrial age, inventions in bread-making machinery and better ingredients began to appear, changing the way bread was made. They also changed how bread was viewed. Commercial yeast and chemical *leaveners* began to appear, and machines such as the steam-powered mixer were invented.

LOAF LINGO

Leavener refers to the substances used to lighten the texture and increase the volume of a substance, such as a dough or batter.

With electricity came electric-powered dough mixers, which could knead dough stronger and faster than by hand, producing airy, voluminous loaves. Powerful and reliable commercial yeasts also became accepted, which began to free the baker from the long process of growing natural yeast starters, or ferments. Fine, white flours with high protein contents also became less expensive and more widely available.

All these innovations combined to create a bread industry that could produce lighter, whiter loaves at a quicker rate than ever before. However, without the long fermentation and heartier grains, many of these newer breads lacked the flavor and nutritional value of the former breads, and quality was lost. People loved these warm and fresh white bread loaves, though, and long-fermented, whole-grain loaves fell out of fashion. Until the artisan revival, that is.

The Bakery Versus Home Baking

Bakeries have been a necessity since the Roman Empire, providing the arena and proper equipment for baking bread that many people lacked. Having a wood-fired clay oven in the home simply wasn't a reality. At times, it was common for the bakery to be a sort of rental space, where customers brought an unbaked loaf to the baker, who would bake the loaf for a fee.

Even with the advent of the electrical appliances we have today, bread still takes time, and it also takes a certain knowledge and craft to do it. And as people are busier today than seemingly ever before with their work and lives, and as bread continues to be widely available in more and more venues, bread-making has, until recently, remained mostly in the hands of the bakers.

Artisan Fever

In the 1980s, people began to take a new interest in the quality of bread they were eating. Recognizing that some of the new ingredients and mixing methods were ultimately producing inferior products, a few bakers began to carve out a "back-to-basics" niche with breads.

These bread-makers resurrected the craft of *artisan bread*-making by building flavor through the process of long ferments and the use of ingredients like whole grains. These old-style breads—with unsurpassed flavor and texture—were finally made new again. Little by little, a growing awareness arose for what we had been missing, and these days more bakers produce artisan breads than ever before.

LOAF LINGO

Artisan bread is bread that's handcrafted rather than mass-produced. Rather than being baked on an assembly line, artisan breads are baked in small batches. Quality ingredients are used, and care and attention are given to the handling of the dough.

And this growing interest in hand-crafted breads didn't stop in the bakery. People began wanting to bake these breads fresh—from their own home. Bread machines have become quite the rage for someone who wants to bake his or her own bread at home, but something is lost in the handcrafted experience when you simply dump ingredients into a machine and press a button.

For those who want to craft their own breads, better methods have been devised so bakers of all kinds can get professional results at home. A portable baking stone that mimics the floor of a clay oven is one great example.

The No-Knead Revolution

The no-knead process has completely revolutionized bread-baking by making hand-shaped artisan breads completely accessible to the home baker. By mixing together a fairly wet dough and allowing it to rest, gluten strands develop on their own. This takes away any need for kneading, whether by mixer or by hand. The dough literally gets stronger on its own. And as the dough sits, great flavor develops. (I explain this fully in Chapter 2.)

By taking advantage of the refrigerator, no-knead doughs have the added advantage of being adaptable to your schedule. The dough can rest in the cool refrigerator for days and baked whenever you're ready to do it.

When you think about it, it seems we have finally caught on to something early humans had figured out—without even knowing it—a long time ago. Ancient man was most likely not breaking his back and kneading bread *at all*. He was probably just letting the mixture sit around until he was good and ready to bake it. Makes sense to me!

The Least You Need to Know

- Early civilizations cooked grains and water to develop flatbread, the first portable convenience food.
- Man soon learned to utilize yeast to make leavened bread.
- The fermentation produces carbon dioxide gas, develops flavor, and contributes to the dough's ability to expand.
- The industrial age impacted how bread was produced, pulling it away from its hand-crafted artisan roots and drawing it closer to mass-produced loaves.
- In the 1980s, a renewed interest began to appear for healthful artisan breads.
- The no-knead method revolutionized the bread-making process.

Baking from Scratch 101

In This Chapter

- A closer look at bread dough
- Kneading and proofing tips
- No need to knead!

It took some time, but baking from scratch seems to be undergoing a revival. While it's hard to ignore the plethora of ready-made, plastic-packaged baked goods, a growing group of home cooks are discovering the joys of baking artisan breads at home. I know you're busy, but that's exactly why no-knead artisan bread recipes fit perfectly into your routine.

Baking from scratch enables you to be a part of the transformation of a few simple ingredients into a delicious loaf of bread. When you make it yourself, you know exactly what's going into it. And unlike wet cake batters or sticky cookie doughs, bread doughs for the most part are tactile and meant to be handled. With bread-baking, it's okay to dig your fingers deep within that bag of soft flour and to sprinkle it all over your table. Feeling the smooth, supple dough as you shape it is rewarding and relaxing—not to mention fun!

Although the principles of bread-making remain the same—mix the dough, let the dough rise, and bake the dough—the main difference between traditional bread methods and the no-knead method is the absence of kneading. In this chapter, I explain how by using the no-knead method, you can make breads with less work than ever before.

Perhaps you've always felt timid when it comes to making bread because you were afraid of making a mistake. Let me put your fears to rest. By the end of this chapter, you'll know all about what a bread dough is and what happens as it transforms from simple ingredients to a loaf. You'll also learn what the dough needs to stay happy so you can avoid errors. Having this knowledge before you start puts you in control. And that's right where you should be.

Bread Dough Basics

Let's start with some dough science. The change from individual ingredients into a dough happens as soon as the ingredients are mixed together. After just a few quick stirs, the mixture becomes a cohesive mass called a dough.

At this point, the starches in the flour have absorbed some of the water. Something else has also begun to take place in the dough: the formation of gluten. Gluten is created from specific proteins in flour called glutenin and gliadin. In dry flour, these proteins are bunched up and separate; but when moistened, they form long, stretchy strands called gluten. You can see this right from the start because the mixed dough will sometimes have a little stretch to it as you finish stirring.

BAKER'S DOZEN

The dough must have enough water in it to moisten all the flour. If at any time you find you've mixed together a dough that still contains pockets of flour, or if the mixture seems really dry and too stiff to stir, add lukewarm water to the dough, 1 tablespoon at a time, until it is moistened.

Two integral processes occur in the dough before it is baked:

- The development of structure in the form of gluten
- The gaseous expansion of the dough

Let's take a closer look at both of these events.

Traditional Kneading

When the ingredients have been combined, the traditional way to develop the gluten is to knead the dough, using either a mixer with a dough hook or by hand. Basically a continuation of stirring, the dough is folded over on itself again and again to create gluten. With this technique, the gluten-forming proteins are moved around until they can align themselves and create a stretchy dough.

The time needed to develop gluten in this way varies, but it's generally about 10 minutes.

Perfect Proofing

The process by which the dough's gases rise and expand is known as *proofing*. Water in the dough activates enzymes in the flour to change the starches into sugars. Yeast love to eat sugar and begin to gobble it up like crazy. As the yeast eat, they grow and give off carbon dioxide gas and alcohol.

LOAF LINGO

Proofing refers to the rest period during which yeast is given time to expand and raise the dough.

Kneading the dough develops the gluten "net" that traps the gases produced from the yeast. The gases inflate the stretchy pockets of gluten, and the overall volume of the dough gets bigger. It may seem like the dough is miraculously creating more dough, but it's just becoming larger because the dough is filling with carbon dioxide and alcohol.

Traditionally, once the dough has been kneaded, it's then placed in a bowl and left alone until it has proofed to approximately double its size. Next, the dough is shaped and then left to proof again before it's baked.

BREAD HEAD

Professional bakers and bread bakeries often use proof boxes. These special pieces of equipment used to proof dough maintain a temperature of around 90°F to 110°F and a humidity of around 90 percent. This allows the bakery to produce consistent bread every time.

The No-Knead Method

The traditional methods of kneading and then proofing are tried and true, but if you don't have a mixer, it takes a bit of effort to knead the dough and then you have to wait the appropriate length of time for the dough to proof and then to bake.

If you're checking your watch and looking through your calendar to see when you'll have time for all this, you're not alone. But I have a solution for you.

Introducing the no-knead method.

This modern-day approach to bread-baking employs a more relaxed technique appropriate for today's busy home cook. By utilizing water and time, no-knead doughs are convenient and easy, and they take the mystery out of bread-baking.

Let the Bread Do All the Work

I know what you're thinking. *It sounds too good to be true!*—but believe me, it's not. You *don't* have to knead dough ever again. With the no-knead method, water and time do all the work for you. Instead of manually pushing the flour proteins around to help them line up, a dough with extra water gives the proteins enough room to move around and align themselves into gluten strands on their own.

Now, to be clear, it's not as if the proteins are floating from one side of the ball of dough to the other. The proteins are in such close proximity to each other that all they need is a little extra space (which they have, thanks to the water) to form a gluten bond with the protein next to it. For the recipes in this book, this will happen in as little as 6 hours.

BREAD HEAD

Scientifically speaking, the process of the flour absorbing the water and allowing gluten to develop on its own without manual manipulation is known as *autolyse.*

If you've made traditional bread before, you might notice that no-knead doughs are softer. While traditional bread recipes avoid incorporating extra flour into the dough when shaping because it could make the bread tough, this isn't the case for no-knead doughs. It's okay to sprinkle ample flour on your hands and work surface in order to handle the dough.

Time Builds Flavor

Once the dough is mixed, it needs to rest on the counter at room temperature so the yeast gases can get going. Depending on the temperature of the room, this takes about 2 or 3 hours. After that, you can slide it into the refrigerator, and in as little as 3 hours, you have a dough that's ready to shape and bake. (The cool temperature helps keep the dough firmer and more manageable.)

Another great advantage to the no-knead method is the concept of a slow ferment. As long as the yeast has a food source, it will continue to thrive and produce gas. A dough that has a longer proof time will have more flavor than a dough with a quick proof time. So because no-knead doughs are rested for an extended period of time to develop gluten, this also gives them more time to develop flavor. Less work, and a tastier bread to boot!

DOUGH DON'T

Remember food safety. Doughs that contain ingredients sensitive to food-borne illnesses, such as eggs, should not be left out to rise on the counter for more than 3 hours.

Leave It Until You Need It

As you familiarize yourself with a few of the no-knead dough recipes later in the book, you'll see that baking bread isn't as strict as it seems. Mix a dough in the morning and bake it that night? Sure! Mix a dough in the morning and bake it 3 days later? Absolutely!

The yeast keeps the dough alive and active. As long as the yeast has enough to feed on and the dough isn't left to dry out, the dough will stay healthy and viable for baking for days. Because of this, no-knead doughs are a great make-ahead food.

Over time, however, the yeast will run out of food and slowly die. When this starts to happen, the dough will, little by little, lose its rising power. A dough that's been left for too long will bake pale and dense, with a heavy alcohol aroma. A dough that gets to this point usually isn't worth eating. Toss it out and start again.

The Least You Need to Know

- While traditional bread-making methods require you to manually manipulate the dough for an extended period of time, all you have to do with artisan bread is leave the dough alone.
- Chilling bread dough for a longer, slower fermentation time develops gluten and flavor—not to mention is much more convenient.

- Preparing dough ahead of time lets you enjoy delicious, fresh-baked bread whenever the craving hits.
- If instructed, allow a second rise at room temperature to create an airy loaf.
- While a dough can wait in the fridge until you're ready to bake, it cannot wait forever. After about a week, the yeast in the dough loses power and the dough won't properly rise.

Know Your Ingredients

In This Chapter

- Choosing your ingredients
- The role of ingredients in artisan breads
- The best ways to measure and store ingredients

A great recipe is one that has the right balance of ingredients. Each ingredient has its special job to do, and it's the reactions of these ingredients that creates the perfect loaf of bread.

The first step in any recipe is to gather your ingredients. Whether choosing a bread made with the barest of ingredients (flour, water, yeast), or with everything but the kitchen sink, each ingredient's contribution to the recipe is important. Starting out with the right ingredients of the highest quality is crucial to the success of your loaf.

In this chapter, I discuss the basic ingredients used in these recipes and each of their roles in the bread-baking process. When shopping, you'll often find many different options for a single ingredient. I share with you which ingredients to avoid and which ingredients you can swap. I also give advice on the proper storage of these ingredients as you begin to stock your pantry.

The All-Important Flour

Flour is the building block of any bread. This essential ingredient gives the bread substance and structure. Yeast feed on the starches in flour, and the proteins form gluten.

Flour is made by grinding dried grains into a powder. It can generally be divided into two types: wheat and nonwheat. The bread recipes in this book primarily use either all-purpose, bread, or whole-wheat flours. Different flours have different protein levels and, thus, varying abilities to create gluten. Because breads rely on a certain amount of gluten development, the amount of protein in the flour affects the outcome of the bread. Knowing these differences can help you understand each flour's ability to create a strong and stretchy dough.

The best place to store flour is in a clean, airtight container in a cool, dry place. If you live in a particularly hot or humid climate, store your flour container in the freezer to protect the flour from moisture and pests.

BAKER'S DOZEN

When measuring flour (or confectioners' sugar or cocoa powder), don't pack the measuring cup. Gently spoon the flour into the cup until it's slightly rounded, and use the back of a butter knife to level it off.

All-Purpose Flour

As the name implies, all-purpose flour is a basic, all-around flour and is generally acceptable in most bread recipes. Milled from the endosperm portion of the wheat kernel, all-purpose flour contains a middle-ground range of protein—about 9 to 12 percent. This percentage of protein gives all-purpose flour enough strength to create the necessary amount of gluten for many of the bread recipes in this book.

You'll find both bleached and unbleached all-purpose flour on your store shelf. If at all possible, steer clear of bleached flour for the no-knead recipes in this book. Chemicals used in the bleaching process reduce the flour's protein content, making it very weak. That's no good for bread recipes, which require a strong, high-protein flour.

Avoid using cake or pastry flour, too, which also have a low-protein content. In general, loaves made with cake, pastry, or bleached flour may not rise properly because they don't have the ability to form enough gluten.

Bread Flour

When it comes to forming gluten, bread flour is a powerhouse. With about 12 to 14 percent protein, this wheat flour has stronger gluten-forming capabilities than all-purpose flour. Because of its strength, bread flour is often used in combination with other flours that contain little or no gluten, such as rye or oat flour.

Bread flour is specifically labeled "bread flour" or "high-gluten flour."

Whole-Wheat Flour

Whole-wheat flour is ground from the entire wheat kernel, including the outer bran coating as well as the germ. This makes whole-wheat flour more nutritious and flavorful than all-purpose or bread flour.

Whole-wheat flour lends a nutty, earthy flavor and a wonderful golden color to breads. It contains less gluten, however, and is generally used in combination with bread flour to give a loaf structure.

Other Flours and Whole Grains

Flours and grains such as rye, oat, cracked wheat, and corn are used in bread recipes for their wonderful flavor and textures. Because these flours or grains contain very low gluten or none at all, they're usually paired with either all-purpose or bread flour so the bread has enough total protein for the gluten to develop. The collaborative effort helps the loaf rise properly.

In general, loaves with these flours and grains are somewhat denser, heartier, more nutritious, and much more intensely flavored than loaves made with all-purpose or bread flour alone.

DOUGH DON'T

Whole-wheat, rye, and oat flours, along with whole grains such as cracked wheat, contain oils from the germ. This makes them more susceptible to spoilage, so store these flours and grains in the refrigerator for a longer shelf life.

How Sweet It Is: Sweeteners

Sweeteners are important for flavoring breads, contributing moisture to baked breads, and also providing some of the food yeast need to grow. However, while yeast thrive on sugar, too much of it isn't a good thing because the yeast become overloaded on the sugar and become slow. Take care if you try to sweeten any of these recipes; they've been developed with the perfect balance of yeast and sugar in mind.

Try not to swap out dry and wet sugars in these recipes. Wet sweeteners such as molasses contribute to the liquid in the recipe and will throw off the total liquid amount. This will make your dough either too loose or too dry, and it may alter the texture of the baked loaf.

Granulated and Confectioners' Sugar

Granulated sugar, or white sugar, is made from sugar cane or sugar beets. Superfine sugar, which is granulated sugar ground finer, may be substituted in a pinch. Because moisture will cause sugar to clump, store your sugar in an airtight container and in a cool, dry place.

Confectioners' sugar, also known as powdered sugar, icing sugar, or 10× sugar, is granulated sugar that's been ground into a powder. Because it's so fine, it dissolves instantly in liquid. This makes confectioners' sugar a good choice for many icing recipes.

In these recipes, granulated sugar and confectioners' sugar should not be used interchangeably because granulated sugar does not have the same dissolving properties as confectioners' sugar.

A small amount of cornstarch added to confectioners' sugar can keep it from lumping, but you may still need to sift it before using if it's particularly lumpy. Be sure to store confectioners' sugar tightly sealed in a cool, dry place.

Brown Sugar

In the past, brown sugar was simply unrefined sugar, which meant it still contained some molasses. Today, it's easier for manufacturers to process and remove the molasses from sugar and then go back and "re-create" brown sugar by adding some of the molasses.

Dark brown sugar has a deeper molasses flavor than light brown sugar. Light and dark brown sugars can be used interchangeably depending on how deeply flavored you'd like your bread to be.

 BAKER'S DOZEN

If you find yourself with a hard brick of brown sugar, don't toss it out! Bring it back to life by heating it in the oven on very low heat for a few minutes until it's just softened. Use it immediately.

When measuring brown sugar, always pack it firmly into the measuring cup, pressing with your hand or a smaller measuring cup and then leveling off the top.

Brown sugar is extremely susceptible to drying out and will become rock-hard if left exposed to air. Always store it in an airtight container.

Molasses

Molasses, the by-product of the boilings of sugar processing, is dark, rich, and a potent flavor-builder in many breads. When choosing molasses for use in bread, opt for unsulfured molasses, which is made from boiling ripened sugar cane juice. It's a high-quality molasses. Sulfured molasses is the by-product of sugar-making and retains some of the sulfurs used in the refinement process.

Blackstrap molasses is the least-sweet of all because it's the end result of the many boilings in the sugar-refinement process.

Honey

Produced naturally by the honeybee, this sweet golden syrup has a distinctive flavor that's closely related to the type of nectar the bee collects and eats. Clover honey, for example, has a mild, floral flavor and is widely available in stores.

Any type of honey will work in these recipes. Experiment and find your favorite!

 BAKER'S DOZEN

Get every bit of sticky sweeteners such as molasses or honey from your measuring cup by first lightly spraying the cup with nonstick vegetable spray. This helps the syrup to slide right out, leaving none of the yummy goodness behind. If oil is used in a recipe, use the measuring cup for the oil first and then the sweetener.

Artificial Sweeteners

Artificial sweeteners have a different chemical makeup than sugar, which may cause the baked product to have a different texture. For most of the yeasted breads, sugar substitutes are fine to use because the amount of sugar in the recipe is fairly small. For quick breads, which have more sugar, you may not get as good a result. Also, not all sugar substitutes are good for baking. Splenda is generally a decent substitute. And be sure the package states whether it can be used for baking, and consult the specific substitution ratios of the product you use.

Enhancing Flavor with Salt

Salt is a mineral that enhances the natural flavor of many of the foods we eat. All the recipes in this book call for table salt, which is readily available.

Be sure you use noniodized salt. In iodized salt, potassium iodide is added as a dietary supplement, but this can leave an off, metallic flavor in the finished bread.

Kosher salt is coarser noniodized salt and can be substituted in any of the recipes in this book. Kosher salt crystals are larger and fluffier and take up more space on a measuring spoon than table salt. So if you use kosher salt in place of table salt, double the amount called for in the recipe.

Too much salt inhibits yeast growth because it interferes with the yeast's ability to take up water. Salt amounts in these recipes have been carefully balanced so take care if you choose to increase the salt in a recipe. Some recipes may instruct you to add particularly salty ingredients, such as olives, at specific times. Follow these instructions as stated. This is purposely done to keep the yeast happy and allow it to work properly while the dough rises.

Leaveners: On the Rise

Leaveners are the ingredients that make breads rise. They transform what would otherwise be a brick-dense, nearly inedible loaf into something that's light, airy, and a delight to eat.

Of all the ingredients listed in this chapter, we've benefited the most from the modern advances in the variety, availability, and consistency of leaveners. Because of this, artisan bread-making at home is more accessible and enjoyable than ever.

Yeast

The yeast used to bake bread is a living organism, *saccharomyces cerevisiae*. This type of yeast feeds on simple sugars. When the yeast is in the dough, it feeds on the starch molecules that have been broken down into sugars. As the yeast feeds, two by-products are formed:

- Alcohol

- Carbon dioxide gas

The creation of carbon dioxide gas expands the dough and gives it rise. The alcohol contributes to the flavor.

 BREAD HEAD

Did you know: 1 pound of yeast contains roughly 3,200 billion yeast cells.

Wild yeast is present in the air around us and is often used in bread-baking by mixing flour with water and allowing it to sit and ferment. This process works but isn't always consistent. If you don't want to take any chances, the most foolproof route is to use commercially made yeast. This is commonly found in the form of active dry yeast and fast-rising, or "instant" yeast. For the recipes in this book, active dry yeast is sufficient, not the fast-acting version. However, it's okay to substitute fast-rising yeast. Compressed, or fresh "cake" yeast is mostly used by commercial and retail bakeries. This yeast is high in moisture and comes in block form. It has a creamy texture and a short shelf life. While home bakers usually prefer to use dry yeast, if you do have fresh yeast on hand, you can substitute 1 tablespoon fresh yeast for every $2^{1}/_{4}$ teaspoons dry yeast.

Be sure to store yeast tightly sealed in the refrigerator to keep it cold and dry. Opened packets of yeast should be wrapped tightly in plastic wrap or sealed in a small zipper-lock bag to prevent it from coming in contact with moisture.

Chemical Leaveners

The introduction of chemical leaveners opened doors in baking like never before. Prior to reliable chemical leaveners, bakers had only yeast or air to use to leaven their breads. Today we have two very popular and reliable chemical leaveners to work with:

- Baking soda

- Baking powder

Baking soda is bicarbonate of soda. When exposed to an acidic ingredient such as buttermilk or sour cream, it releases carbon dioxide gas, which will leaven, or raise, the baked product.

Baking powder takes this one step further. Baking powder is a mixture of bicarbonate of soda *plus* an acid (such as cream of tartar or calcium phosphate). Because it includes the acid in the powder, no additional acid is needed in the recipe. When the baking powder is moistened and exposed to the heat of the oven, it goes to work by producing carbon dioxide and leavening the baked good.

The difference between single-acting and double-acting baking powder is simple. Single-acting baking powder releases carbon dioxide as soon as it's moistened. Double-acting needs both moisture and heat to react completely.

Air

Air? As a leavener? You bet. And you don't need anything more than elbow grease to use air as a leavener in a dough or batter. As you beat or whip eggs, yolks, or whites, pockets of air become contained in a network of proteins, which, when baked, stretch and set, holding the air within.

In the quick bread recipes, eggs and sugar are beaten slightly to incorporate a small amount of air into the batter to help lighten the loaf.

Make Friends with Fats

Fats are important to bread recipes because they not only contribute flavor, but they also tenderize. When flour is coated with a fat, it cannot form gluten strands as easily because the fat blocks the proteins from reacting with water. In recipes where an especially chewy bread is desired, fat is kept to a minimum.

A few different types of fat are used in these recipes:

- Olive oil

- Vegetable oil

- Butter

Olive oil, extracted from pressed olives, produces superior flavor and is used in many savory bread recipes. While extra-virgin olive oil has the most flavor, regular olive oil is perfectly acceptable.

Made from veggies such as corn, vegetable oil has a neutral flavor and is used in recipes where the tenderizing qualities of the fat are wanted. Canola oil, made from the rapeseed (a member of the mustard family), is a good, neutral-flavored vegetable oil to use. Vegetable shortening is another fat that can be used when a neutral flavor is desired.

Butter contributes lots of flavor and is used primarily in quick bread recipes. Use unsalted butter for the recipes in this book. It's difficult to judge the amount of salt a salted butter contributes in a recipe, and it can produce inconsistent flavor results. If you only have salted butter on hand, you can omit the other salt from the recipe, but the final flavor may still be off.

DOUGH DON'T

Avoid using margarine in bread-baking. It not only produces an off taste, but also contains trans fatty acids, which are extremely unhealthy to consume.

Excellent Eggs

Eggs are crucial to the structure of a bread that hasn't developed significant gluten, such as a quick bread. Here, the proteins in the eggs set in the heat of the oven, forming a matrix throughout the batter, which holds the bread together. However, in most yeast breads, enough gluten has been developed to hold the bread together, and eggs are added mostly for richness.

The addition of eggs also helps tenderize bread because of the fat in the egg. You can also brush egg over bread before it goes into the oven for a loaf with a shiny, golden glaze.

The recipes in this book call for large eggs. Either brown or white eggs will do. There's no difference in flavor.

Wonderful Water

Water is without a doubt one of the most crucial elements in the no-knead bread process. A wet dough with ample water provides the necessary room for the gliadin and glutenin proteins to move around and align themselves into stretchy gluten strands. It also allows the yeast plenty of room to move around, consume sugars, and release carbon dioxide gas, which expands the gluten strands.

When the loaf is in the oven, water in the form of steam steps up to the plate. The steam keeps the surface of the dough soft enough to expand properly. The water on the surface also promotes a crisp crust because it helps the starch enzymes convert to sugar, which caramelizes and crisps in the oven, turning the crust into a tasty and crunchy golden brown.

> **BREAD HEAD**
>
> The temperature of the water you add to the dough is critical to the survival of the yeast. Never add hot water because yeast begins to die at 120°F. It kills your yeast. Lukewarm is best. The best way to tell if the temperature is lukewarm is to touch it. If it barely feels warm, it's okay.

You don't have to go out and purchase special water for these recipes. Regular tap water will do just fine, unless your tap water has an off taste.

Bring on the Dairy

Dairy products contribute water, fat, flavor, and sometimes acid to a dough. Many forms of dairy products are used throughout the no-knead artisan bread recipes.

When choosing milk, any type will do, although whole milk has the richest flavor. Sour cream, yogurt, and buttermilk will add a zingy tang to recipes. And the acid in these dairy ingredients also reacts with baking soda, as when used for making many of the quick breads.

> **BAKER'S DOZEN**
>
> If you don't have buttermilk, you can make your own by combining 1 cup milk with 1 tablespoon white vinegar or lemon juice. Let it stand for about 10 minutes or until it begins to thicken.

In a few recipes, nonfat dry milk powder is called for. This ingredient adds intense flavor. Liquid milk in place of the water in the recipe is an acceptable substitute.

Adding Some Flavorings

Now for the ingredients added for extra flavor. Feel free to experiment with flavorings after you get comfortable with the recipes. Keep in mind, however, that ingredients that are particularly vinegary or salty, such as olives, may inhibit the production of yeast if used in large amounts. If you like your breads with more olives than the amount given, you can experiment with larger amounts.

Dried fruit has been dehydrated to remove much of the moisture to help preserve it. These fruits include raisins, currants, cherries, figs, dates, and tomatoes. For some of the recipes, I re-hydrate the fruit to plump it back up. Feel free to exchange any dried fruit in a recipe to suit your taste.

BREAD HEAD

Scientifically speaking, a tomato is a fruit because it develops in the ovary of the flower and contains the seeds of the plant. Other fruits often thought of as vegetables include beans, eggplant, bell peppers, and squash.

Alcohol is a by-product of yeast fermentation, so it makes sense that a bit of beer will aid in the overall yeasty and fermented flavor of a bread. Stick with milder ales, which lend good flavor without being too bitter. Remember, though, that beer also contributes to the liquid in the recipe.

Vinegar, produced by fermenting such liquids as in cider, wine, or beer, is astringently acidic. When added to bread dough, it enhances flavor by reinforcing the sour notes that normally occur in yeast fermentation. Common vinegars include cider, wine, and malt.

Nuts add texture and flavor to bread. Feel free to interchange nuts in the recipes to suit your personal tastes. Lightly toasting nuts before using them increases their flavor and crunchy texture. While nuts are high in fat, they're also very nutritious because they contain protein, vitamins, and calcium. The oils in nuts can spoil quickly, and nuts tend to absorb odors, so to keep them fresh for as long as possible, store nuts tightly wrapped in the freezer.

When it comes to spices, a small amount goes a long way in terms of flavor. Spices come from dried seeds, berries, or bark. The recipes in this book generally call for easy-to-find dried ground spices. You can also grind your own fresh spices, such as nutmeg, by using a Microplane grater or a spice grinder. The flavor of a freshly ground spice is more intense, so adjust the amount used by a pinch. Store spices in a cool, dry spot to preserve them for as long as possible. Old spices lose their potency and take on musty flavors.

Herbs, the tender leaves of plants, add lots of fresh-from-the-garden flavor to breads. Some herbs such as cilantro and dill can be particularly sandy, so be sure to thoroughly wash your herbs before using them. Simply let them soak in a big bowl of water. The herbs will float to the top and the sand will sink to the bottom.

The Least You Need to Know

- Before you begin to bake, be sure to measure out all your ingredients first.
- Each ingredient is important to the recipe. Substitutions may affect the final outcome.
- Choose high-quality ingredients for the best results.
- Store your ingredients properly to maintain freshness.

Your Tools

In This Chapter

- Essential bread-making tools and equipment
- Tips using and caring for your tools
- The all-important oven

A few simple pieces of equipment and utensils are all you need to begin baking fresh, no-knead artisan bread. And because many of these tools are useful in other baking and cooking applications, you may already have them in your kitchen.

As with any tool, the more you use it, the more comfortable you'll become with it. Pretty soon you'll be whirling around your kitchen like a pro, and the local kitchen store may become a favorite hangout as you scope out your next newest kitchen tool!

The number of baking supplies available these days can make it difficult to determine what you *really* need. To help you out, this chapter's list of equipment and tools represents the core basics for no-knead bread-baking. You can find many of these items in the cooking and baking aisles of department stores, but be sure to look in Appendix B for additional sources.

Sheets and Stones

Your beautiful dough is risen and ready, and now you have to place it on or in something to bake. What the dough is baked on affects how heat is transferred to the loaf during baking. This helps create that delectable crunchy bottom on your loaf of bread.

Aluminum sheet pans are one of the most useful pieces of equipment in restaurants and bakeries, and you'll soon find they're handy in your home bakery, too. Most common is the 13×18-inch size, which is also known as a *half-sheet pan.* The rimmed edges on these pans make them useful for baking focaccia and for preventing some foods, such as soda bread or biscuits, from slipping off onto the floor. Sheet pans are also useful as a holding pan for water when baking breads that benefit from steam to create a crunchy crust. Some pans are coated with a nonstick surface, but it's generally not preferred, as these are easily scratched over time. Also, if the nonstick surface is dark, it will conduct too much heat and burn the bottom of your bread.

Cookie sheets are usually lip free and are also generally made of aluminum. Look for a pan that's heavy duty and not nonstick.

Pizza stones, also known as baking stones, are ceramic squares that mimic the baking surface of a professional stone oven. Pizza stones are about 14×14 inches and about $^1/_2$ inch thick. Rye breads, pizzas, and baguettes are baked directly on the stone, usually with some cornmeal sprinkled on the stone to help prevent sticking. The ceramic material helps wick away moisture from the loaf, ensuring a crisp and crackling crust. Because the stone is absorbent, avoid washing it with soap and water; you want to keep it dry. Simply scrape off any debris that's collected on the stone. Some people just leave the stone in the oven during the oven's cleaning cycle to keep it clean. If you don't have a baking stone, you can still bake bread on a baking sheet, but the crust won't turn out as crisp. Alternatively, just about everything can be baked on a pizza stone, with the exception of focaccia.

DOUGH DON'T

To get the most benefit from a baking stone, preheat the stone in your oven for about 30 minutes to get it good and hot before baking your loaf. And be careful! Not only does the stone get super-hot, it retains the heat for a very long time. Be sure it's sufficiently cooled down before handling or moving it to storage.

Pots and Pans

Just as with baking pans and stones, pots and pans can affect the final crust texture of the loaf, as well as its shape. While certain loaves rely on a specific pot for optimum texture, recipes that call for the loaf to be baked in a molded pan are less rigid. For pans such as a loaf or brioche mold, let loose and experiment with different shapes!

And not just for the stove, certain pots, such as Dutch ovens, are equally at home in the oven. Don't just place any pot in the oven, though. Be sure it's labeled "oven safe."

Not actually an oven, *Dutch ovens* are pots usually made of either cast iron or heavy-duty aluminum and stainless steel. Very often these are ceramic coated. Dutch ovens are especially useful when baking round boules because the pot encloses the steam and creates an ovenlike atmosphere that produces an especially crisp crust.

Loaf pans enable you to bake the doughs that are too wet to hold their own shape, such as sandwich breads and quick breads. Look for a pan that's Pyrex or heavy-duty nonstick aluminum. A nonstick pan is preferable to help release the loaf from the pan after baking. A 8$^{1}/_{2}$×4$^{1}/_{2}$×3-inch loaf pan works best. A 9×5×3-inch pan also works, but it results in a shorter, squattier loaf. If you do use a 9×5×3-inch pan, you may need to subtract a few minutes from your baking time.

Bundt pans are deep, round, tube-shape pans, generally with decorative scalloped sides that produce a pretty molded bread. While these pans are commonly used to bake Bundt cakes, they're also useful when baking wet doughs such as babka or kringle. While a Bundt pan generally holds a larger volume of dough than a typical loaf pan, its tubular shape helps the dough bake evenly.

Fluted brioche molds help create the perfect shape to a classic brioche bread. They are easily found in kitchen stores and online. They come in an assortment of sizes and the nonstick variety is especially convenient.

Other Equipment

While some of the pieces of equipment in this section are specific to baking artisan breads, most are commonly used kitchen tools you might already have in your cupboard. In any case, they're important to have on hand. These tools will make mixing and handling the dough a breeze.

Pizza Peel

You may have seen a pizza peel in use at your local pizzeria. This flat tool is used to help slide your bread or pizza on and off the baking stone. It has a long handle to help keep your hands safely away from the hot baking stone. Luckily, smaller versions are available for home ovens. If you don't have a pizza peel, you can use a cookie sheet that doesn't have a rimmed edge.

Proofing Baskets

Proofing baskets offer an easy way to deal with wetter no-knead doughs. They are ideal for creating decorative designs on round loaves such as boules. They also enable you to give your dough a longer final proof before baking, which helps produce a lighter crumb. The traditional proofing basket, called a *brotform*, has a round, bowl-like shape. It usually has an indented pattern on the inside of the bowl, which gives the finished loaf a professional-looking design.

Using a proofing basket is simple. Be sure your proofing basket is well floured to prevent sticking. After using, knock out the excess flour but don't wash the bowl. When you're ready to bake, form the dough into a round shape and place the dough back in the basket with the seam side up. Allow the dough to rest for about 30 minutes, and transfer the dough to a preheated Dutch oven by quickly and carefully flipping the dough out of the basket and into the pot. If the dough doesn't land in the center of the pot, you can try shaking the pot to center the dough or use a wooden spoon to adjust its position.

To turn the dough into the Dutch oven, grasp both sides of the proofing basket and flip the dough into the pot so the decorative side is on top.

Thermometers

You've invested your time preparing a loaf of bread for the oven, so don't let your oven—or your loaf—sabotage you! Correct oven temperature is essential for baking no-knead breads and having an oven thermometer is the best way to know your oven is correctly calibrated.

Bread baked in an oven that's too low won't get the proper lift. And bread baked in an oven that's too hot won't rise either because the surface sets before the dough has had a chance to fully expand. Sometimes this creates a "burst" top on the bread where the dough is trying desperately to escape. A hot oven also causes the exterior of the bread to brown and burn before the interior is cooked through.

BREAD HEAD

If you find your oven is off, you can either consult your oven manual to reca-librate the oven or simply adjust the temperature dial until the thermometer registers the correct temperature.

No less important than an oven thermometer is a probe thermometer. This type of thermometer allows you to take your loaf's temperature. Because breads often develop a hard, crisp, golden crust before the interior is baked, sometimes you can be misled into thinking the loaf is done. Instant-read thermometers are especially handy because they give an almost instant digital readout.

Measuring Cups and Spoons

Baking is a science, and successful baking begins with correct measurements. Unlike some cooking recipes, you can't eyeball your way through a baking recipe. This makes the use of measuring cups and spoons absolutely imperative. If you're the kind of person who thrives on structure, measuring out your *mise en place* will be right up your alley! Be sure you have the following on hand for use in baking:

- A dry cup measurement set
- A set of measuring spoons
- At least one 8-ounce liquid measuring cup with markers

LOAF LINGO

Mise en place is a cooking term every culinary student learns the very first day. It means to gather, measure out, and prep all your ingredients into bowls before you start to bake or cook.

As a general rule, use dry cup measures for dry ingredients, and liquid cup measures for all liquids. When measuring a liquid, be sure to read the measurement at eye level because standing above a liquid measure gives you an incorrect reading.

The recipes in this book always call for flat level measurements, never rounded. Inaccurate measuring could radically change the flavor and texture of your bread. The one exception is with flavorings such as spices. If you really like a lot of spice or herb flavor, tossing in a little extra is perfectly fine. I do it all the time.

Nonstick Baking Liners

Nonstick baking liners make any baking surface nonstick—and make cleanup a cinch! A liner can be as simple as a piece of disposable parchment paper, which is readily available at the supermarket and sold in rolls.

Flexible silicon baking mats are a great investment because they can be washed and reused. They can also be put in the refrigerator, freezer, and microwave. A nonstick silicone mat is made of woven glass fibers coated in silicone. These mats can withstand oven temperatures of up to 500 degrees Fahrenheit. The glass fabric provides excellent temperature conduction, and silicone is a nonstick material.

Scrapers, Knives, and Other Miscellaneous Tools

We're almost done with the must-have list of tools and equipment you'll need for bread-baking. Just a few more small but mighty tools ....

First up, *dough scrapers.* Dough scrapers are made from a stiff but flexible plastic. They enable you to efficiently scrape every last bit of sticky dough from bowls. Once you start using this useful tool, you'll wonder how you lived without it.

And no professional baker is without a *bench knife.* Bench knives are made of a hard, thin metal that's not as sharp as a regular knife but is rigid enough to cut and portion bread doughs with ease. Bench knives are extremely useful to scoop up prepped ingredients from cutting boards, and they're indispensable when scraping dough from work surfaces.

Next, *pastry brushes.* These small brushes are used to gently brush the tops of breads with a glaze or egg-and-water mixture before baking.

DOUGH DON'T

Pastry brushes that aren't cared for properly can harbor bacteria, so be sure to always wash the brush well with soap and water after each use, rub your hand across the brush to separate the bristles before drying, and dry the brush with the bristles pointing up.

Bread knives are serrated and are very efficient utensils for cutting slices of bread. The sawlike blade cuts through even the softest of breads without crushing the tender crumb.

Rulers are helpful for leveling off dry measurements and are essential for creating consistent and professional-looking portions of dough. (Variously sized pieces of dough bake at different rates, making determining doneness difficult later on.)

A *loaf tester* is used to check a loaf's doneness. For many breads, the best way to check for doneness is with a thermometer, but items that are long and thin can be used to see if the center is still doughy. Long wooden skewers; metal skewers; toothpicks; or even long, thin, knives will work.

Used mostly for the quick bread recipes, a *whisk* combines ingredients very efficiently. A whisk is also useful to incorporate air, such as when making whipped cream.

An *offset spatula* has a dull metal blade that's attached to a handle at an angle that makes it particularly useful for reaching under items. The angled blade also makes spreading icings a cinch. These spatulas come in a multitude of sizes. You can usually find them in kitchen stores or online.

A *zester* helps you shred away the outer peel of a citrus fruit. Many different tools can accomplish this, including a simple box grater, but I've found that the most effective tool is a Microplane. Find one online or in kitchen gadget stores.

Finally, get yourself a *cooling rack*. Usually made of a thick wire mesh, cooling racks help prevent a soggy crust by allowing steam to escape from under the bottom of the bread as it cools.

Your Oven

Your oven is where the magic of baking comes to fruition as your raw ingredients are transformed into delicious loaves of bread. Now, I don't expect you to go out and buy a new oven specifically for bread-baking, but a few basics might help you understand the connection between your oven and delicious no-knead bread.

Both gas and electric ovens work equally well. Whichever oven you have, it's important to properly preheat the oven before baking your breads. This can take anywhere from 10 to 30 minutes, depending on your particular oven, so be sure you have an oven thermometer in place before you begin. Before preheating, adjust the oven rack to the correct position (indicated in the recipe), and place the baking stone and sheet pan (if using) on their respective racks. Unless otherwise noted in the recipe, the oven rack should be in the middle position.

Most ovens have hot spots, specific areas in the oven that are hotter and brown foods quicker. If your oven is browning one part of your bread faster than the rest, be sure to rotate the bread so it bakes evenly. In most situations, turning the bread once about halfway through baking is sufficient.

Most ovens, especially gas or older models, use traditional still-air heat, but yours may be equipped with a convection option. Some microwaves also have a convection switch. Convection baking uses a fan to circulate the heat around the oven. This results in hotter, faster baking that isn't suitable for most of the bread recipes in this book. The exterior will brown too quickly and the loaf will look done before the interior has cooked through. Convection baking is better reserved for items such as biscuits and scones that have faster baking times. For these smaller items, baking temperature and times are given for still-air ovens, so if you choose to use convection, decrease the temperature slightly and use your best judgment to determine when it's done.

The Least You Need to Know

- Baking sheets and pizza stones can be used interchangeably; however, pizza stones produce the thickest and crustiest bread bottoms.
- Proofing baskets are an optional but recommended tool for baking round loaves.
- Accurate measuring is essential in order to turn out perfect breads.
- The temperature at which you bake your bread is crucial. Know your oven.

Mixing, Resting, and Baking

5

In This Chapter

- Incorporating the ingredients
- Caring for your dough
- The baking process
- Storing breads and planning ahead

Now that you've read all about baking from scratch, know what ingredients you need, and have all your tools in hand, it's time to put it all together. In this chapter, I take you through the processes of no-knead artisan bread-baking, from the raw ingredients to the final baked loaf, explaining each method used for the recipes in this book so you can become familiar with each step.

Understanding the different methods used (instead of blindly following steps), means you have more control and helps you be a successful baker. It also helps you catch yourself before you make any mistakes!

Mixing Things Up

A few terms are used to refer to specific actions you perform when combining ingredients. Each has a different effect on the final texture.

Stirring involves simply mixing together your ingredients until they're combined. A wooden spoon or a rubber spatula works best for this. Recipes specify whether to stir until smooth or stir until "just moistened." In some recipes, too much stirring begins to produce gluten and results in a tough bread. If the instructions say to just moisten, stir until you don't see any more dry pockets of flour. A few lumps are okay and don't need to be smoothed out.

Whisking is generally used to combine eggs and sugar in a quick bread recipe. Whisking traps air into the eggs and sugar, which helps leaven the quick bread in the oven. As the quick bread bakes, steam causes these air pockets to expand before the batter sets, creating a lighter texture in the final baked bread.

To use a whisk, quickly stir together the ingredients to combine. The thin wires of the whisk help incorporate and trap air within the egg and sugar mixture. As air is incorporated, the mixture will lighten slightly in color. Don't whisk too far in advance because over time, the air will escape and the mixture will deflate.

The purpose of *whipping* is to add volume and incorporate even more air into an ingredient than by simply whisking and lightening. For the purposes of this book, whipping is only required for making whipped cream topping. When you're whipping an ingredient, you know you're done when you've reached the "peak stage." This can either be a soft or stiff peak. For a whipped cream topping, a soft peak is best. To determine the soft peak stage, lift the whisk out of the bowl after whisking and hold the whisk upright. If the tip of the whipped cream droops over to the side slightly, you've achieved a soft peak. Soft peak is the recommended stage for the recipes in this book. You'll know you've whipped the cream a little too much if you've reached stiff peak. This is when the whipped cream holds a stiff shape when you lift the whisk from the cream.

BAKER'S DOZEN

To get the most volume when whipping cream, always start with a cold bowl and whisk. Place the bowl and whisk in the refrigerator for 1 hour before whipping.

If you've ever wondered how croissants get their incredible flakiness, the answer is *lamination*. This method incorporates butter by layering it into such doughs as croissants, Danishes, and puff pastries. It may sound complicated, but laminating is easily accomplished. Begin by spreading butter onto a rolled-out piece of dough. Fold the dough over into thirds and then roll out again. You'll repeat this process a few more times. Each time you fold and roll out the dough, layer upon layer of butter is encased in the dough. When the dough is baked, heat causes the steam in the butter to expand, creating delicate, flaky layers.

When laminating a dough, the temperature of both the butter and the dough is very important. The dough must be well chilled so it's firm enough to take the butter spread over it, and the butter must be just soft enough to spread over the dough without ripping it. The butter can't be too soft, however, or it will melt into the dough and the layering of butter and dough won't be achieved.

Time Out for Resting and Rising

Resting and rising are both integral to the success of a no-knead bread. Both steps happen at the same time.

Giving dough a chance to rest does a few things. First, it gives the yeast in yeast breads a chance to grow, or *proof*. The gases resulting from this growth expand and rise the dough, and the dough also develops flavor.

Second, and most important for no-knead doughs, resting gives the proteins in the flour time to unravel and re-link into strong gluten strands. Without sufficient resting, no-knead doughs wouldn't work.

In no-knead breads, there are four resting and rising steps.

Stir and Sit

The first rest and rise occurs just after the dough is stirred together. At room temperature, the live yeast becomes activated in the dough's moist environment that's also loaded with food, and it begins to grow. As the yeast grows, yeasty flavor begins to develop and it expels gases, which in turn begin to stretch and expand the dough.

It's important to let the dough rise in a bowl or container that's at least 4 quarts capacity. Cover the bowl or container loosely (usually with a piece of plastic wrap) to prevent the dough from drying out and developing a hard skin on the surface of the dough. If the dough develops this skin, it will make it difficult for the dough to expand.

Speaking of expansion, growing yeast knows no boundaries, and if you don't have the proper container, you may leave your kitchen only to come back to a flowing, volcaniclike mess all over your counter!

You'll know the dough has completed its first rise when it's about doubled in size and is bubbly all over the top. This usually takes about 2 or 3 hours.

Chill Out

The second rest and rise occurs in the refrigerator. This is also known as *slow rising*, or *retarding the dough*. In this cold environment, the yeast continues to grow but at a slower pace, all the while the gluten continues to form and strengthen.

Resting the dough at this point is a crucial step in no-knead bread-making that cannot be skipped or even rushed. I like to think of it as a well-deserved beauty rest for your loaf. A sufficient rest is required for stretchy gluten to develop in the dough.

Unless otherwise noted in the recipe, no-knead dough is generally rested in the refrigerator for 3 to 24 hours before the next step.

> **BAKER'S DOZEN**
>
> Don't leave the dough uncovered in the refrigerator! It will form a hard skin on the surface and begin to dry out. No-knead doughs need to be kept moist for the process to work.

A special bonus of no-knead dough is that after it has rested its minimum amount of time in the fridge, you don't have to feel rushed to immediately take it out to bake. No-knead bread dough can rest in the refrigerator for a day or even two if you don't have time to work with it again immediately. Longer rests increase the yeasty, fermented flavor of the bread, which you may prefer. However, as the dough is stored longer, the yeast starts to lose its power and the loaf won't rise as much when it's baked.

Refrigerating the dough is especially helpful to no-knead dough because the cool temperature helps firm the wet no-knead dough, making it easier to shape than a room-temperature dough.

Shape and Sit

The next step occurs just after the dough is shaped. Letting the dough sit at room temperature gives the chilled dough a chance to rise again before it's baked, ultimately contributing to a light and airy crumb.

During rising, you want the dough to maintain a temperature of about 70°F to 80°F. If it's summer, or if you live in a particularly warm climate, you may want to place the dough in a cooler spot in the house, such as by a nearby air-conditioner vent.

Knowing when the dough is ready for the oven can feel like a tricky step because under- or overproofing the dough at this point will affect the final texture of the bread. To tell when a pan loaf dough is ready to be baked, gently poke it with your finger. If an indentation remains on the dough's surface, the loaf is ready to be baked.

After the long rest in the refrigerator, the dough will be cold. Allowing the dough to warm up a bit (roughly 30 minutes), lets it rise to full capacity in the oven. Conversely, letting the dough rise too much before baking isn't a good thing. You don't want to wait too long before baking the bread. If left out on the counter for too long, the yeast will soon peter out. The result will be a bread that initially rises in the oven but then falls, leaving you with a deflated and sad-looking loaf.

DOUGH DON'T

It's important to note that not all the no-knead doughs in this book get this second rest before baking. Some of the wetter doughs and boules are shaped and then immediately baked. Otherwise, they would be too fragile to handle. A proofing basket is a great tool for this because it allows you to let the dough rise without having to handle it later.

Spring Up

The last rise is the bread's final hurrah in the oven. Typically known as *oven spring*, this is where the heat of the oven creates steam to help expand all the pockets of air in the dough and the yeast give their last burst of energy before the heat of the oven kills them.

For chemically leavened quick breads, there's only one rise. This occurs in the oven.

Shaping and Slashing the Dough

As mentioned earlier, after the dough has rested in the refrigerator, it's ready to be shaped. This step determines the final look of your bread. Because no-knead doughs are particularly wet, you'll want to dust your work surface and your hands with enough flour to keep the dough from sticking to your hands or your work surface while you shape it.

BAKER'S DOZEN

If your hands begin to get sticky with dough, simply adding more flour to them won't prevent more sticking. Instead, wash and dry your hands thoroughly and then dust them with new flour.

Slashing is not only decorative, but is also beneficial to proper baking. Many of the doughs require a few shallow slashes in the top of the loaf just prior to baking, either with a knife or kitchen shears. This breaks any skin that may have developed on the surface of the dough, which could hinder the loaf from expanding to its fullest in the oven. If the loaf isn't slashed, it might also split in places that aren't attractive, causing an exploded appearance. Instructions are given in each recipe for slashing your loaf, but ultimately, you can be creative with your own designs.

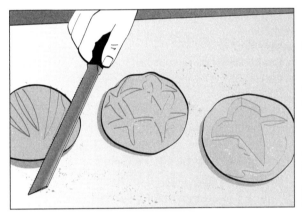
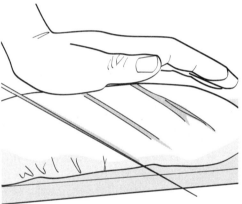
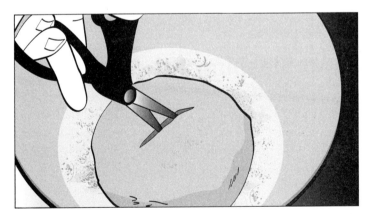

Slashing your loaf, either with a knife or kitchen shears, adds a decorative element as well as helps the bread expand as it bakes.

Adding Heat

In this final step, the oven's heat transforms the dough into delicious bread. Many things happen all at once during this step. Heat inspires the leaveners to kick into full gear for one last rise. Heat also creates steam from the moisture in the dough, which expands air pockets, creating lift. This is known as oven spring. As the dough bakes, proteins begin to set, creating a solid and stable structure. And surface starches in the crust are converted to flavorful sugars.

Baking Time and Temperature

Baking times are given for each recipe, but because ovens, pans, and ingredients may vary, use the baking times as close approximations, not absolutes. Visually inspect the loaf, feel the top, and check with a thermometer or skewer to judge doneness. Trust your common sense when deciding when to remove a loaf from the oven.

That said, it's very important to retain a consistent temperature in the oven while the loaf bakes, so although it might be tempting, try to avoid opening the oven door to peek at your loaf until the bread is nearing the end of baking.

Is It Done?

You've gotten this far and it's time to pull the loaf from the oven. It looks golden, but how can you be sure it's ready? Certainly a lot rides on this step because after putting in your time and effort (not to mention ingredients), you want your bread to emerge perfect. And there's nothing worse than cutting into a loaf with a gooey center.

Because no-knead breads are moister than kneaded breads, it's a little difficult to really overbake the loaf, which is a good thing. An overbaked loaf, however, is not a total loss. It'll still make great toast or breadcrumbs.

If you follow the recipe directions, the loaf will usually be done within a few minutes of the suggested time. The loaf will be golden, crisp, and set. To know for certain if the loaf is ready, I recommend taking the loaf's temperature. When the loaf looks done, insert a probe thermometer into the center of the loaf. Most of the loaves in this book are finished baking anywhere from 190°F to 210°F.

DOUGH DON'T

Most breads are finished baking at a temperature that's on the cusp of 212°F, which is the point water starts turning to steam and evaporates out of the loaf. Avoid baking your bread past this point, or your loaf will begin to get dry.

If you don't have a thermometer, you can get a pretty good (although not foolproof) idea if the center is thoroughly baked by inserting a skewer into the center of the loaf. You want the skewer to come out clean or with just a few moist crumbs. If the skewer comes out doughy, the loaf needs more baking.

After the Bake Is Over

Wait! Once you remove the fresh baked loaf from the oven, there are a few things to keep in mind before you dig in. These will help ensure the loaf has the best texture.

The aroma of freshly baked bread is intoxicating, making it almost impossible to resist tearing off a warm hunk as soon as it's out of the oven. While I can't exactly say I've always practiced what I preach (it's embarrassing to admit, but I've been known to eat almost half of a warm loaf in one sitting), I do recommended you wait until the bread completely cools before cutting into and eating it. The moisture in the bread needs time to distribute evenly. If you cut the loaf too soon, lots of steam will escape prematurely, and that will affect the final texture. Some loaves are impossible to resist eating warm, however, and that's just one of the wonderful joys of artisan baking.

BREAD HEAD

Cooling bread on a cooling rack allows for proper ventilation of the bottom crust.

How you store your bread affects how well it keeps. (Although after discovering how delicious homemade bread is, you may not even need to know how to store it at all because it'll disappear so quickly!) The best way to keep bread fresh is to place it on a cutting board with the cut end sealed with plastic wrap, or loosely place the loaf in a paper bag with some holes poked through. You want to allow some airflow around the bread to keep the crust from getting soggy. Storing the loaf in the refrigerator causes the bread to go stale sooner. And avoid storing the loaf in an airtight plastic bag.

Par-Baking

Par-baking is a method of partially baking the bread, storing it, and then finishing baking it at a later time. It's a great method to use if you want to keep an emergency loaf stored away to be available at a moment's notice. Because of their size, boule breads work best for this method, but you can also experiment with other breads.

To par-bake a bread, first bake the loaf until it's about $^3/_4$ of the way through the baking time. For a boule, this would be approximately 5 minutes after the lid has been removed from the Dutch oven. You want the center to be just about cooked but before the crust has completely browned. The temperature of the center should be around 180°F. Take the loaf out to cool completely, wrap tightly with plastic wrap or place in a zipper-lock bag/freezer bag, and store it in the freezer.

When you're ready to finish baking, you can use a couple methods, depending on the size of the bread. For a par-baked round loaf, place the frozen loaf in a Dutch oven that's been heating in a 450°F oven, and bake with the lid on for about 5 minutes. Remove the lid and finish baking until the crust is golden and crisp. For a longer loaf, or rolls, place the bread on a baking sheet and then place in a preheated 400°F oven for approximately the rest of the time needed to bake the bread stated in the recipe or until golden and crisp.

The Least You Need to Know

- Incorporating your ingredients properly is a crucial part to achieving a great-tasting bread.
- By refrigerating the dough, you can control when the loaf will be baked.
- The best way to know when bread is done baking is to probe it with a thermometer. Most breads are done between 190°F and 210°F.
- Although delicious eaten just out of the oven, a bread will have its best texture after it has cooled completely.

Yeast Breads

Few aromas are more recognizable than that of a baking yeast bread. Savory yeast breads are the heart and soul of the baking world. Before sugar, chemical leaveners, or fancy flavorings came along, people lived off breads made from three essential ingredients: flour, yeast, and water. These simple ingredients have formed the foundation from which all other breads have sprung. As you bake your way through the following chapters, you'll see how versatile yeast bread is and how many ways it can be incorporated into a nutritious meal.

In the chapter on boules, you'll learn the technique of baking in a pot. This is one of the best and newest methods for getting a crunchy crust on your artisan bread. With loaf pan breads, the pan shapes the loaf for you. To help you get comfortable with the no-knead method, these breads are a good place to start.

The remaining chapters advance your baking skills as I introduce you to new techniques. Long, rustic loaves make use of a baking stone, which mimics the bottom of a clay oven. The flatbread, pizza, and focaccia chapter shows how easy it is to make a hearty, complete meal out of a no-knead bread. I've also included recipes for breads you may have never thought you could make at home, such as bagels and pita pockets. The easy instructions make these recipes approachable.

Boules

In This Chapter

- Basic boules
- Hearty whole-grain boules
- Sourdough boules
- Sweet and savory boules

Boule (pronounced *BOOL*), may sound like a fancy word, but it's simply just the French word for ball. When a loaf of bread is called a boule, it's because the loaf is round. Boules are some of the easier and most satisfying breads to make because they require hardly any shaping, yet in the end, you're rewarded with a beautiful loaf that looks like it was just pulled from a brick oven. The boule shape is one of the most ancient shapes in bread-making, so when you make these breads, you're participating in a ritual that's thousands of years old.

The recipes in this chapter cover basic boules, which need just a few simple ingredients, as well as heartier, whole-grain boules. You can even surprise your family at the dinner table with a savory Chocolate-Cherry Boule!

The most important thing to remember is that these loaves are supposed to be rustic looking. Imperfections in shape and size are okay! The loaf will still be absolutely delicious.

A Pot O' Bread

One of the big secrets to getting crusty, no-knead artisan boules at home is a heavy-duty cast-iron Dutch oven. When a boule is baked in a Dutch oven with the lid on, a "microclimate" is created inside the pot. This climate traps all the escaping steam from the dough and helps the dough to rise and then form that bakery-fresh crackly crust. A little over halfway through baking, you remove the lid, and the bread is allowed to bake to a golden crisp.

When baking with a Dutch oven, place it on a rack that keeps the pot near the middle of the oven. This is usually a lower-middle rack. To get the most benefit from the pot, preheat it in the oven for at least 30 minutes. I find it easiest to place the empty pot in the oven when I turn on the oven to preheat.

When it comes time to transfer the dough from the mixing bowl or work surface to the pot to bake, be careful because the pot will be *very* hot! Always give the bottom of the pot a good sprinkling of cornmeal to help prevent the boule from sticking. Once the dough has been placed in the pot, it shouldn't really be moved around at all. If you wind up placing the dough in the pot a little off to the side, you can try to gently shake the pot a little to center it or use a wooden spoon to nudge it into place. And don't forget to put the lid back on!

BREAD HEAD

Using a Dutch oven produces great crunchy, chewy boules, but you can also bake the bread on a baking stone or even a baking sheet. The results might not be quite as crusty, though.

Shaping Your Boule

Shaping a piece of dough into a round boule is easy. No-knead doughs tend to be stickier than regular doughs, so be sure to keep your hands and work surface well floured. Using your hands, simply shape the dough into a ball and then place it into the pot.

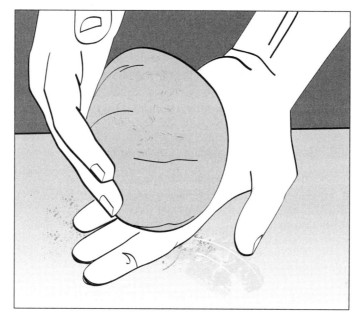

Using well-floured hands, gather the dough on the work surface and cup it in your hands. Gently roll the dough around, using the tension of the dough on the board to help tighten it. Tuck any seams underneath the ball as you place it in the pot.

Classic French Boule

The quintessential French boule, this loaf has a fairly even *crumb* with some craggy holes.

Yield:	Prep time:	Rest and rise time:	Cook time:	Serving size:
1 (8-inch-round) loaf	10 minutes	6 to 24 hours	1 hour	1 (½-inch) slice

3½ cups plus 1 TB. all-purpose
  flour

1½ tsp. salt

1¼ tsp. instant or rapid-rise yeast

1¼ cups lukewarm water

2 TB. yellow cornmeal

1. In a large bowl, stir together 3½ cups flour, salt, and yeast. Stir in water until completely combined and no white pockets of flour remain.

2. Loosely cover with plastic wrap and let rise at room temperature for 2 or 3 hours or until dough has doubled in size and surface is covered with large bubbles.

3. Refrigerate dough for at least 3 hours, or preferably overnight.

4. Place a Dutch oven on the lower-middle oven rack, and preheat the oven to 425°F for 45 minutes.

5. On a well-floured work surface and with well-floured hands, shape dough into a 6-inch-round ball.

6. Sprinkle cornmeal in the bottom of the Dutch oven. Carefully transfer dough ball to the Dutch oven, seam side down, and sprinkle the top with remaining 1 tablespoon flour. With a sharp knife, make 2 or 3 shallow slashes in top of loaf. Immediately place the lid on top of the Dutch oven.

7. Bake for 40 minutes and then remove the lid. Continue to bake for about 20 more minutes or until crust is a deep golden brown and a thermometer inserted into the middle of loaf registers about 210°F.

8. Cool for 30 minutes in the Dutch oven with the lid off. Carefully transfer loaf to a cooling rack to cool completely. Cut into slices and serve.

LOAF LINGO

You'll see the word **crumb** often referred to when describing a baked item. It's simply a way of defining the texture of the baked item. For example, a cake may have a fine and tender crumb, but a bread may have an open, chewy crumb.

Cracked Whole-Wheat Boule

This is the bread to turn to when you crave something hearty and wholesome. The nutty cracked wheat adds chewy texture.

Yield:	Prep time:	Rest and rise time:	Cook time:	Serving size:
1 (8-inch-round) loaf	1 hour	6 to 24 hours	1 hour	1 (½-inch) slice

½ cup *wheat berries,* chopped

1 cup boiling water

2 cups whole-wheat flour

1 cup plus 1 TB. bread flour

2 tsp. yeast

1¾ tsp. salt

3 TB. honey

½ cup plus 2 TB. lukewarm water

2 TB. cornmeal

1. Place wheat berries in a small bowl, and pour boiling water over the top. Allow to cool completely.

2. In a large bowl, stir together whole-wheat flour, 1 cup bread flour, yeast, and salt. Stir in cooled wheat berry mixture, honey, and lukewarm water until completely combined.

3. Loosely cover with plastic wrap and let rise at room temperature for 2 or 3 hours or until dough has doubled in size and surface is covered with large bubbles.

4. Refrigerate dough for at least 3 hours, or preferably overnight.

5. Place a Dutch oven on the lower-middle oven rack, and preheat the oven to 450°F for 45 minutes.

6. On a well-floured work surface and with well-floured hands, shape dough into a 6-inch-round ball.

7. Sprinkle cornmeal in the bottom of the Dutch oven. Carefully transfer dough ball to the Dutch oven, seam side down, and sprinkle the top with remaining 1 tablespoon flour. With a sharp knife, make 2 or 3 shallow slashes in top of loaf. Immediately place the lid on top of the Dutch oven.

8. Bake for 40 minutes and then remove the lid. Continue to bake for about 20 more minutes or until crust is a deep golden brown and a thermometer inserted into the middle of loaf registers about 210°F.

9. Cool for 30 minutes in the Dutch oven with the lid off. Carefully transfer loaf to a cooling rack to cool completely. Cut into slices and serve.

LOAF LINGO

Wheat berries are the entire wheat kernels. They're hard, so they usually need to be soaked before using to slightly soften them.

Walnut-Date Boule

Dense and chewy, the coarsely chopped walnuts and sweet dates make this loaf particularly hearty and satisfying.

Yield:	Prep time:	Rest and rise time:	Cook time:	Serving size:
1 (8-inch-round) loaf	1 hour	6 to 24 hours	1 hour	1 (½-inch) slice

1 cup dried dates, chopped

1 cup boiling water

2 cups whole-wheat flour

1¼ cups bread flour

1¼ tsp. yeast

1¼ tsp. salt

¾ cup lukewarm water

1 cup toasted walnuts, roughly chopped

2 tsp. honey

2 TB. cornmeal

1. Place dates in a medium bowl, and pour boiling water over the top. Allow to cool completely.

2. In a large bowl, stir together whole-wheat flour, bread flour, yeast, and salt. Stir in lukewarm water, walnuts, honey, and date mixture until completely combined.

3. Loosely cover with plastic wrap and let rise at room temperature for 2 or 3 hours or until dough has doubled in size and the surface is covered with large bubbles. Refrigerate dough for at least 3 hours, or preferably overnight.

4. Place a Dutch oven on the lower-middle oven rack, and preheat the oven to 450°F for 45 minutes.

5. On a well-floured work surface and with well-floured hands, shape dough into a 6-inch-round ball. Work in more flour if dough is too sticky to shape into a ball. Let dough ball rest on work surface for about 30 minutes to come to room temperature.

6. Sprinkle cornmeal on the bottom of the Dutch oven. Carefully transfer dough ball to the Dutch oven, seam side down. With a sharp knife, make 2 or 3 shallow slashes in top of loaf. Brush top of loaf with water. Immediately place the lid on top of the Dutch oven.

7. Bake for 40 minutes and then remove the lid. Continue to bake for about 20 more minutes or until crust is a deep golden brown and a thermometer inserted into the middle of loaf registers about 210°F.

8. Cool for 30 minutes in the Dutch oven with the lid off. Carefully transfer loaf to a cooling rack to cool completely. Cut into slices and serve.

Make it your own: If dates aren't your thing, you can substitute an equal amount of chopped dried figs.

BREAD HEAD

Dates, harvested from the date palm tree, have been cultivated since ancient times. They are valued for their high sugar content, which gives them a sticky, candy-sweet flavor, and their texture when dried. Look for pitted dates when shopping.

Sourdough Starter

This yeasty mixture gives sourdough bread its signature tangy flavor. (Note: In this book, I've only used this starter for the sourdough, but you could add it to other breads.)

Yield:	Prep time:
1½ cups	3 to 6 days

¾ cup all-purpose flour   ¾ cup lukewarm water

¼ tsp. yeast

1. In a medium container with a lid, stir together 2 tablespoons flour, yeast, and 2 tablespoons water. Cover with the lid and allow to sit at room temperature for about 1 hour.

2. Refrigerate overnight.

3. The next day, stir in 2 tablespoons flour and 2 tablespoons water until completely combined. Refrigerate overnight.

4. Continue to stir in 2 tablespoons flour and 2 tablespoons water for at least 3 days, refrigerating overnight. At 3 days, starter may be used for baking, but it gets better with each passing day.

BREAD HEAD

Keeping a sourdough starter is like keeping a pet. To care for it, you must feed the yeast with flour and water. As long as you regularly replenish the starter with a few tablespoons of flour and water so it has the consistency of a thick batter, it will keep almost indefinitely in the fridge.

Sourdough Boule

This chewy loaf has a beautiful crunchy round dome and a moist, custard-y crumb. The starter sponge gives this loaf a deep, rewarding flavor.

Yield:	Prep time:	Rest and rise time:	Cook time:	Serving size:
1 (8-inch-round) boule	20 minutes	6 to 24 hours	70 minutes	1 (½-inch) slice

3¼ cups plus 1 TB. bread flour

1½ tsp. yeast

1½ tsp. salt

½ cup Sourdough Starter (recipe earlier in this chapter)

1¼ cups lukewarm water

2 TB. cornmeal

1. In a large bowl, stir together flour, yeast, salt, Sourdough Starter, and water until completely combined.

2. Loosely cover with plastic wrap and let rise at room temperature for 2 or 3 hours or until dough has doubled in size and surface is covered with large bubbles.

3. Refrigerate dough for at least 3 hours, or preferably overnight.

4. Place a Dutch oven on the lower-middle oven rack, and preheat the oven to 450°F for 45 minutes.

5. On a well-floured work surface and with well-floured hands, shape dough into a 6-inch-round ball. Let rest on work surface for about 30 minutes to come to room temperature.

6. Sprinkle cornmeal in the bottom of the Dutch oven. Carefully transfer dough ball to the Dutch oven, seam side down, and sprinkle the top with remaining 1 tablespoon flour. With a sharp knife, make 2 or 3 shallow slashes in top of loaf. Immediately place the lid on top of the Dutch oven.

7. Bake for 45 minutes and then remove the lid. Continue to bake for about 25 more minutes or until crust is a deep golden brown and a thermometer inserted into the middle of loaf registers about 210°F.

8. Cool for about 30 minutes in the Dutch oven with the lid off. Carefully transfer loaf to a cooling rack to cool completely. Cut into slices and serve.

Make it your own: For quick sourdough flavor without the starter, you can substitute ½ cup plain yogurt and add 2 tablespoons fresh lemon juice for the starter.

BREAD HEAD

A true sourdough bread doesn't use commercial yeast but instead relies entirely on wild yeasts that occur naturally. But this method can sometimes be inconsistent. I inject my starter with a little commercial yeast to help get it going.

Whole-Wheat Sourdough Boule

This bread's wonderful nutty flavor comes from whole-wheat flour.

Yield:	Prep time:	Rest and rise time:	Cook time:	Serving size:
1 (8-inch-round) loaf	20 minutes	6 to 24 hours	70 minutes	1 (½-inch) slice

2 cups whole-wheat flour

1¼ cups plus 1 TB. bread flour

1½ tsp. yeast

1½ tsp. salt

½ cup Sourdough Starter (recipe earlier in this chapter)

1½ cups lukewarm water

3 TB. honey

2 TB. yellow cornmeal

1. In a large bowl, stir together whole-wheat flour, bread flour, yeast, salt, Sourdough Starter, water, and honey until completely combined.

2. Loosely cover with plastic wrap and let rise at room temperature for 2 or 3 hours or until dough has doubled in size and surface is covered with large bubbles.

3. Refrigerate dough for at least 3 hours, or preferably overnight.

4. Place a Dutch oven on the lower-middle oven rack, and preheat the oven to 450°F for 45 minutes.

5. On a well-floured work surface and with well-floured hands, shape dough into a 6-inch-round ball. Let dough ball rest on work surface for about 30 minutes to come to room temperature.

6. Sprinkle cornmeal in the bottom of the Dutch oven. Carefully transfer dough ball to the Dutch oven, seam side down, and sprinkle the top with remaining 1 tablespoon flour. With a sharp knife, make 2 or 3 shallow slashes in top of loaf. Immediately place the lid on top of the Dutch oven.

7. Bake for 45 minutes and then remove the lid. Continue to bake for about 25 more minutes or until crust is a deep golden brown and a thermometer inserted into the middle of loaf registers about 210°F.

8. Cool for 30 minutes in the Dutch oven with the lid off. Carefully transfer loaf to a cooling rack to cool completely. Cut into slices and serve.

BAKER'S DOZEN

I've called for making slashes in the top of the dough to help the boule expand while it bakes, but feel free to be creative and create your own pattern! Maybe try a spiral or cross-hatching.

Chocolate-Cherry Boule

Dark and crusty, deep undertones of cocoa form the base of this moist, hearty bread that's dotted with sweet and tangy dried cherries.

Yield:	Prep time:	Rest and rise time:	Cook time:	Serving size:
1 (8-inch-round) loaf	10 minutes	6 to 24 hours	70 minutes	1 (½-inch) slice

3 cups all-purpose flour

½ cup unsweetened cocoa powder

3 TB. firmly packed light brown sugar

1½ tsp. salt

1¼ tsp. yeast

1½ cups lukewarm water

1 cup dried cherries

2 TB. yellow cornmeal

1 batch Cornstarch Baker's Glaze (recipe in Chapter 15)

1. In a large bowl, stir together flour, cocoa powder, brown sugar, salt, and yeast. Stir in water and cherries until completely combined.

2. Loosely cover with plastic wrap and let rise at room temperature for 2 or 3 hours or until dough has doubled in size and surface is covered with large bubbles.

3. Refrigerate for at least 3 hours, or preferably overnight.

4. Place a Dutch oven on the lower-middle oven rack, and preheat the oven to 450°F for 45 minutes.

5. On a well-floured work surface and with well-floured hands, shape dough into a 6-inch-round ball. Work in more flour if dough is too sticky to shape into a ball. Let dough ball rest on work surface for about 30 minutes to come to room temperature.

6. Sprinkle cornmeal in the bottom of the Dutch oven. Carefully transfer dough ball to the Dutch oven, seam side down, and brush with Cornstarch Baker's Glaze. With a sharp knife, make 2 or 3 shallow slashes in top of loaf. Immediately place the lid on top of the Dutch oven.

7. Bake for 40 minutes and then remove the lid. Continue to bake for 25 to 30 more minutes or until crust is a dark brown and a thermometer inserted into the middle of loaf registers about 210°F.

8. Cool for 30 minutes in the Dutch oven with the lid off. Carefully transfer loaf to a cooling rack to cool completely. Cut into slices and serve.

BAKER'S DOZEN

Due to the dark appearance of this bread, it can be difficult to judge when it's done, so a thermometer is really handy here. If you don't have one, insert a long skewer into the center of the loaf. If it comes out clean or with just a few crumbs, it's done.

Potato, Garlic, and Cured Black Olive Boule

This bread is packed with the flavor of olive oil, garlic, and salty, cured black olives. Mashed potato makes this bread especially moist and gives it a unique shape that's flatter than most boules.

Yield:	Prep time:	Rest and rise time:	Cook time:	Serving size:
1 (9-inch-round) loaf	1 hour	6 to 24 hours	70 minutes	1 (½-inch) slice

1 russet potato

2 cups plus 1 TB. bread flour

2 tsp. yeast

1¾ tsp. salt

1½ cups lukewarm water

2 TB. extra-virgin olive oil

1 cup all-purpose flour

½ cup pitted and chopped cured black olives

6 cloves garlic, minced

2 TB. yellow cornmeal

1. Place cleaned and unpeeled potato in a medium saucepan, and fill with enough water to cover potato by at least 1 inch. Cover pot and bring to a boil over medium-high heat, and cook potato for about 30 minutes or until it's easily pierced with a knife. Remove potato, cool, and then gently mash with a fork. Set aside.

2. In a large bowl, stir together bread flour, yeast, and salt. Stir in water and olive oil until completely combined.

3. Loosely cover with plastic wrap and let rise at room temperature for about 2 or 3 hours or until dough has doubled in size and surface is covered with large bubbles.

4. Stir all-purpose flour, olives, garlic, and mashed potato into dough until combined.

5. Refrigerate dough for at least 3 hours, or preferably overnight.

6. Place a Dutch oven on the lower-middle oven rack, and preheat the oven to 450°F for 45 minutes.

7. On a well-floured work surface and with well-floured hands, shape dough into a 7-inch-round ball. Let dough ball rest on work surface for about 30 minutes to come to room temperature.

8. Sprinkle cornmeal in the bottom of the Dutch oven. Carefully transfer dough ball to the Dutch oven, seam side down, and sprinkle the top with remaining 1 tablespoon flour. With a sharp knife, make 2 shallow slits across top of bread. Immediately place the lid on top of the Dutch oven.

9. Bake for 45 minutes and then remove the lid. Continue to bake for about 25 more minutes or until crust is a deep golden brown and a thermometer inserted into the middle of loaf registers about 210°F.

10. Cool for 30 minutes in the Dutch oven with the lid off. Carefully transfer loaf to a cooling rack to cool completely. Cut into slices and serve.

Make it your own: If you prefer, you can replace the garlic with ¼ cup finely chopped onion and replace the olives with ¼ cup chopped fresh dill. And 1¼ cups left-over mashed potatoes are an excellent substitute for the russet potato.

BAKER'S DOZEN

If you can't find oil-cured olives already pitted, you can easily pit them yourself with a small paring knife. Carefully slice the olive to the pit, and with your fingers, squeeze out the pit.

Long and Rustic Loaves

In This Chapter

- Stone and steam matters
- Shaping secrets
- Basic long loaves
- Hearty deli favorites

When I was a child, every Sunday started with a trip to the German bakery in town to pick up a hot, fresh loaf of tangy rye bread so we would have bread to make sandwiches for lunch. It seemed out of the question to even try to bake this type of loaf in a home oven. But with a few basic tools, you—yes, you!—can pull off a beautiful, bakery-style long loaf.

The rustic loaves in this chapter are a variety of styles and shapes, from thin French baguettes to long and low olive and pumpernickel breads. If you've already tried your hand at some of the boules in Chapter 6, then these loaves promise to satisfy your artisan bread cravings even more. Nothing will make you feel more like a true baker than sliding a long loaf onto a hot baking stone with a pizza peel. And you'll delight when you pop open the oven door to find a golden, shiny, and perfectly shaped loaf ready to be scooped out. Your friends and family will be impressed and amazed.

And I guarantee you'll find your pizza peel so useful that you'll want to find a handy spot to hang it so it's within easy reach.

The Three Amigos

A Dutch oven pot conveniently and effectively creates a "mini-oven" environment for boule loaves (see Chapter 6), but the pot is much too small to fit longer loaves like those in this chapter. So to create that perfect baking environment for long artisan breads, three pieces of equipment will become your best friends:

- A baking stone
- A broiler tray
- A pizza peel

The baking stone, made of clay, wicks away moisture from the bottom of the bread, which helps create a crunchy bottom crust. The broiler tray is used to catch water and create steam, similar to professional steam-injected ovens. Without the airtight environment of a Dutch oven, this extra steam is needed to help the loaves expand and create a crisp crust. The pizza peel is indispensable when it comes to sliding loaves into and out of the oven. (Not to mention it looks cool!) Always be sure to sprinkle the peel liberally with cornmeal to help prevent the wet no-knead doughs from sticking.

DOUGH DON'T

If you don't have a broiler tray, or your oven isn't set up with one, *never* resort to pouring water on the bottom of the oven. The change in temperature from the evaporating water can cause warping and damage to the oven. Instead, just place a baking sheet on the bottom shelf below the baking stone.

Shaping the Dough

Shaping a long loaf may seem intimidating, but there's really nothing to it. Simply form the dough into a round shape and then elongate it into an oval with tapered ends, like a stretched-out football. If the dough is especially sticky, just sprinkle with enough flour to make it manageable.

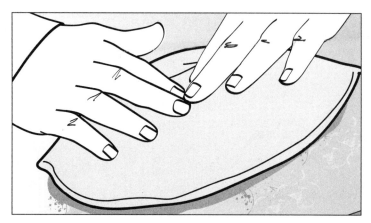

To shape a long loaf, start by rolling the dough back and forth from a round shape to an oval. Applying gentle pressure, slowly stretch your hands farther apart until the loaf is the length you want. Apply more pressure to taper the ends.

To shape a baguette, begin by rolling the dough into an oval shape; keep rolling your hands back and forth as you stretch the dough into a long, thin baguette shape.

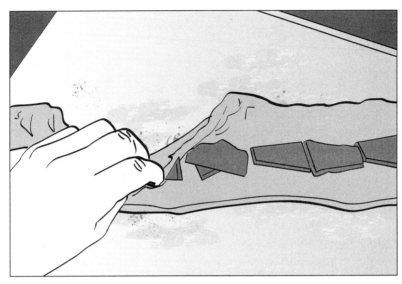

Roll the baguette shape flat with a rolling pin. Place chocolate along the length and then fold the dough over, pinch to seal, and gently roll back into a baguette shape.

Transfer Tips

After you've transferred the dough to the prepared pizza peel and it's ready to go into the oven, slide the loaf onto the hot stone by placing the peel at the far end of the stone, slightly angle the peel, and slide the loaf onto the stone using a few quick motions.

> **BAKER'S DOZEN**
>
> Because no-knead doughs are on the wetter side, sometimes they want to stick on the pizza peel instead of transfer to the stone. If this happens, use a bench knife or long spatula to gently nudge the dough away from the peel and onto the stone. Once the dough is on the stone, you can use the bench knife to gently get it back into shape if it's slightly misshapen. Just be mindful of the hot stone!

Italian Semolina Loaf

Durum flour and a sprinkling of sesame seeds add a hearty and complex flavor to this great all-purpose loaf.

Yield:	Prep time:	Rest and rise time:	Cook time:	Serving size:
1 (14-inch) loaf	10 minutes	6 to 24 hours	40 minutes	1 (2-inch) slice

1½ cups bread flour

1 cup all-purpose flour

½ cup *semolina* flour

4 TB. sesame seeds

2 TB. dry milk powder

2 tsp. yeast

1½ tsp. salt

1½ cups lukewarm water

1 TB. unsalted butter, melted

¼ cup cornmeal

1. In a large bowl, stir together bread flour, all-purpose flour, semolina flour, 2 tablespoons sesame seeds, milk powder, yeast, and salt. Stir in water and melted butter until completely combined.

2. Loosely cover with plastic wrap and let rise at room temperature for 2 or 3 hours or until dough has doubled in size and surface is covered with large bubbles.

3. Refrigerate dough for at least 3 hours, or preferably overnight.

4. Place a broiler tray on the bottom oven rack. Place a baking stone on the lower-middle rack, and preheat the oven to 450°F for 45 minutes. Sprinkle a pizza peel with cornmeal.

5. On a well-floured work surface and with well-floured hands, shape dough into an oblong loaf shape about 12 inches long and 3 inches wide. Work in more flour if dough is too sticky to shape into a loaf.

6. Transfer loaf to the pizza peel. Brush loaf with water, and sprinkle with remaining 2 tablespoons sesame seeds. With a sharp knife, make 3 or 4 shallow diagonal slashes in top of loaf.

7. Slide loaf onto the baking stone. Pour ½ cup hot water into the broiler tray, and immediately close the oven door. Bake for about 40 minutes or until loaf is golden brown and a thermometer inserted into the middle of loaf registers about 210°F.

8. Using the pizza peel, remove loaf from the baking stone and place on a cooling rack to cool completely. Cut into slices and serve.

Make it your own: This bread is perfect for making garlic bread. Simply slice a cooled loaf in half lengthwise and brush the inside with a mixture of 12 tablespoons melted butter, 2 tablespoons minced garlic, 2 tablespoons fresh chopped parsley, and ½ teaspoon salt. Close the loaf, wrap in foil, and reheat in a 350°F oven for 20 minutes before serving.

LOAF LINGO

Semolina is the ground endosperm of milled durum wheat. If you can't find semolina flour, durum flour is a fine substitute.

Lotta Kalamata Olive Bread

Wonderfully crusty on the outside and moist on the inside, this bread is chock-full of briny olive flavor.

Yield:	Prep time:	Rest and rise time:	Cook time:	Serving size:
1 (13-inch) loaf	15 minutes	6 to 24 hours	50 minutes	1 (2-inch) slice

2 cups bread flour

1¹/₂ tsp. yeast

³/₄ tsp. salt

1¹/₄ cups lukewarm water

¹/₄ cup extra-virgin olive oil

1¹/₂ cups all-purpose flour

1 cup pitted kalamata olives, chopped

6 cloves garlic, minced

¹/₃ cup cornmeal

1 batch Essential Egg Wash (recipe in Chapter 15)

1. In a large bowl, stir together bread flour, yeast, and salt. Stir in water and olive oil until completely combined.

2. Loosely cover with plastic wrap and let rise at room temperature for 2 or 3 hours or until dough has doubled in size and surface is covered with large bubbles.

3. Stir all-purpose flour, olives, and garlic into dough. Refrigerate for at least 3 hours, or preferably overnight.

4. Place a broiler tray on the bottom oven rack. Place a baking stone on the lower-middle rack, and preheat the oven to 450°F for 45 minutes. Sprinkle a pizza peel with cornmeal.

5. On a well-floured work surface and with well-floured hands, shape dough into an oblong loaf shape about 11 inches long and 3 inches wide. Work in more flour if dough is too sticky to shape into a loaf.

6. Transfer loaf to the pizza peel. Lightly brush with Essential Egg Wash, and with a sharp knife, make 3 or 4 shallow diagonal slashes across top of loaf.

7. Slide loaf onto the baking stone. Pour ¹/₂ cup hot water into the broiler tray, and immediately close the oven door. Bake for about 50 minutes or until loaf is golden brown and a thermometer inserted into the middle of loaf registers about 210°F.

8. Using the pizza peel, remove loaf from the baking stone and place on a cooling rack to cool completely. Cut into slices and serve.

BREAD HEAD

A garlic press makes easy work of mincing garlic. To use, simply place a garlic clove in the small hopper and squeeze the handle. The garlic is pressed through the grate and ready to use. Be sure to clean the press well immediately after using. If you wait too long, the sticky garlic will dry and be difficult to wash off.

Pain au Chocolat (Bread with Chocolate)

Rich, dark chocolate is baked right into the center of this long, crunchy French bread loaf. Cut into it while it's still warm to enjoy the gooey chocolate surprise.

Yield:	Prep time:	Rest and rise time:	Cook time:	Serving size:
1 (14-inch) loaf	10 minutes	6 to 24 hours	40 minutes	1 (2-inch) slice

2 cups bread flour	6 TB. lukewarm water
2¹/₂ tsp. sugar	2 TB. vegetable shortening, melted
1¹/₂ tsp. yeast	2 oz. bittersweet chocolate
1 tsp. salt	¹/₄ cup cornmeal
¹/₂ cup whole milk	

1. In a large bowl, stir together flour, sugar, yeast, and salt. Stir in milk, water, and melted shortening until completely combined.

2. Loosely cover with plastic wrap and let rise at room temperature for 2 or 3 hours or until dough has doubled in size and surface is covered with large bubbles.

3. Refrigerate dough for at least 3 hours, or preferably overnight.

4. Place a broiler tray on the bottom oven rack. Place a baking stone on the lower-middle rack, and preheat the oven to 450°F for 45 minutes. Sprinkle a pizza peel with cornmeal.

5. On a well-floured work surface and with well-floured hands, shape dough into a long loaf shape 12 inches long and 2 inches wide. Pat down the length of dough to flatten it slightly so it's about 3 or 4 inches wide. Place pieces of chocolate along one side of the length of loaf and fold over loaf, pinching the ends to seal. Gently roll loaf back into a cylinder shape.

6. Gently transfer loaf to the pizza peel, seam side down. Let rest for about 15 minutes.

7. Just before baking, with a sharp knife, make 4 or 5 shallow diagonal slits across top of loaf.

8. Slide loaf onto the baking stone. Pour $^1/_2$ cup hot water into the broiler tray, and immediately close the oven door. Bake for about 40 minutes or until loaf is crisp and golden brown.

9. Using the pizza peel, remove loaf from the baking stone and place on a cooling rack to cool. Cut into slices while slightly warm or let cool completely.

BAKER'S DOZEN

Take my word for it: it's well worth it to use a high-quality bittersweet chocolate in this bread. I like to use Ghirardelli and Callebaut. The chocolate can be in bar, chip, or chunk form, as long as it's evenly spaced along the loaf so there's no arguing over who got the piece with the most chocolate!

Caraway-Rye Loaf Bread

Supremely chewy, this robust bread boasts deli-style piquant flavor, thanks to the cider vinegar.

Yield:	Prep time:	Rest and rise time:	Cook time:	Serving size:
1 (13-inch) loaf	10 minutes	6 to 24 hours	50 minutes	1 (1/2-inch) slice

2 cups bread flour

4 TB. caraway seeds

1 TB. sugar

2 tsp. salt

1 1/2 tsp. yeast

1 1/2 cups lukewarm water

3 TB. cider vinegar

2 cups rye flour

1/4 cup cornmeal

1 batch Cornstarch Baker's Glaze
(recipe in Chapter 15)

1. In a large bowl, stir together bread flour, 3 tablespoons caraway seeds, sugar, salt, and yeast. Stir in water and cider vinegar until completely combined.

2. Loosely cover with plastic wrap and let rise at room temperature for 2 or 3 hours or until dough has doubled in size and surface is covered with large bubbles.

3. Stir rye flour into dough. Refrigerate for at least 3 hours, or preferably overnight.

4. Place a broiler tray on the bottom oven rack. Place a baking stone on the lower-middle rack, and preheat the oven to 425°F for 45 minutes. Sprinkle a pizza peel with cornmeal.

5. On a well-floured work surface and with well-floured hands, shape dough into an oblong loaf shape 12 inches long and 3 inches wide. Work in more flour if dough is too sticky to shape into a loaf.

6. Transfer loaf to the pizza peel. Brush top of loaf with Cornstarch Baker's Glaze, and sprinkle with remaining 1 tablespoon caraway seeds. With a sharp knife, make 4 or 5 shallow diagonal slits across top of loaf.

7. Slide loaf onto the baking stone. Pour 1/2 cup hot water into the broiler tray, and immediately close the oven door. Bake for about 50 minutes or until loaf is golden brown and a thermometer inserted into the middle of loaf registers about 210°F.

8. Using the pizza peel, remove loaf from the baking stone and place on a cooling rack to cool completely. Cut into slices and serve.

BREAD HEAD

Contaminated rye was at the heart of the 1692 Salem witch trials in Massachusetts. A few unlucky colonists consumed ergot-infected rye, which caused them to convulse and hallucinate. This frightened the town and incited a mad witch hunt that ultimately persecuted many innocent people.

Pumpernickel Bread

Rye flour, cocoa, and molasses give this hearty bread its deep, dark flavor—a perfect pairing with it's soft, chewy crust.

Yield:	Prep time:	Rest and rise time:	Cook time:	Serving size:
1 (13-inch) loaf	10 minutes	6 to 24 hours	50 minutes	1 (^{1}/$_2$-inch) slice

2^1/$_2$ cups rye flour

1^1/$_2$ cups bread flour

3 TB. unsweetened cocoa powder

3 TB. caraway seeds

2 tsp. yeast

1^3/$_4$ tsp. salt

1^1/$_2$ cups lukewarm water

4 TB. molasses

3 TB. cider vinegar

2 TB. vegetable oil

^{1}/$_4$ cup cornmeal

1 batch Cornstarch Baker's Glaze (recipe in Chapter 15)

1. In a large bowl, stir together 1^1/$_2$ cups rye flour, bread flour, cocoa powder, 2 tablespoons caraway seeds, yeast, and salt. Stir in water, molasses, cider vinegar, and vegetable oil until completely combined.

2. Loosely cover with plastic wrap and let rise at room temperature for 2 or 3 hours or until dough has doubled in size and surface is covered with large bubbles.

3. Stir remaining 1 cup rye flour into dough. Refrigerate for at least 3 hours, or preferably overnight.

4. Place a broiler tray on the bottom oven rack. Place a baking stone on the lower-middle rack, and preheat the oven to 425°F for 45 minutes. Sprinkle a pizza peel with cornmeal.

5. On a well-floured work surface and with well-floured hands, shape dough into an oblong loaf shape 12 inches long and 3 inches wide. Work in more flour if dough is too sticky to shape into a loaf.

6. Transfer loaf to the pizza peel. Brush top of loaf with Cornstarch Baker's Glaze, and sprinkle with remaining 1 tablespoon caraway seeds. Let dough rest for about 30 minutes. With a sharp knife, make 4 or 5 shallow diagonal slits across top of loaf.

7. Slide loaf onto the baking stone. Pour $^1/_2$ cup hot water into the broiler tray, and immediately close the oven door. Bake for about 50 minutes or until loaf is dark brown and a thermometer inserted into the middle of loaf registers about 210°F.

8. Using the pizza peel, remove loaf from the baking stone and place on a cooling rack to cool completely. Cut into slices and serve.

Make it your own: Add $^2/_3$ cup raisins to the dough in place of the caraway seeds for a sweeter taste.

BAKER'S DOZEN

This pumpernickel bread is delicious sliced and served with Cream Cheese Spread (recipe in Chapter 15).

French Baguette

Crusty and chewy, the only thing missing with this baguette is the long paper bag to put it in when you pluck it from the oven.

Yield:	Prep time:	Rest and rise time:	Cook time:	Serving size:
1 (12-inch) baguette	10 minutes	6 to 24 hours	40 minutes	1 (2-inch) slice

³/₄ cup all-purpose flour	¹/₂ tsp. yeast
³/₄ cup bread flour	³/₄ cup plus 1 TB. lukewarm water
³/₄ tsp. salt	¹/₄ cup cornmeal

1. In a large bowl, stir together all-purpose flour, bread flour, salt, and yeast. Stir in water until completely combined.

2. Loosely cover with plastic wrap and let rise at room temperature for 2 or 3 hours or until dough has doubled in size and surface is covered with large bubbles.

3. Refrigerate for at least 3 hours, or preferably overnight.

4. Place a broiler tray on the bottom oven rack. Place a baking stone on the lower-middle rack, and preheat the oven to 450°F for 45 minutes. Sprinkle a pizza peel with cornmeal.

5. On a well-floured work surface and with well-floured hands, shape dough into a long loaf shape 12 to 14 inches long and about 2 inches wide.

6. Gently transfer baguette to the pizza peel, and sprinkle with flour. With a sharp knife, make 5 shallow diagonal slashes on top of baguette.

7. Slide baguette onto the baking stone. Pour ¹/₂ cup hot water into the broiler tray, and immediately close the oven door. Bake for about 40 minutes or until baguette is crisp and golden brown.

8. Using the pizza peel, remove baguette from the baking stone and place on a cooling rack to cool completely. Cut into slices and serve.

BAKER'S DOZEN

When shaping the baguette, it helps to twist the long piece of dough as you gently roll and stretch it into the baguette shape. This recipe also easily doubles to produce two baguettes.

Loaf Pan Breads

In This Chapter

- Classic loaf pan breads
- Wholesome, good-for-you loaves
- Big-flavor loaves

Many of the breads in this chapter represent the type of loaves you probably grew up eating, and some might bring back memories of brown-bag school lunch days. The big difference here is that no presliced and bagged supermarket loaf can compare to the quality and freshness of a homemade bread made with natural ingredients. And with the no-knead method, it's easier than ever to create oven-fresh versions of all your favorite sandwich-style loaves. From classic white, to whole-wheat, cinnamon-raisin, and honey-oatmeal breads, I've covered the basics with the recipes in this chapter. The Brioche and a dark and moist root beer bread offer more decadent choices.

Because loaf pan breads tend to be on the softer side, they're ideal for times when you don't want a super-chewy bread. Loaf pan breads also keep their wonderful texture day after day, and every single one of these recipes makes to-die-for toast!

It's All in the Pan

One advantage to baking sandwich-style breads is that they require minimal equipment. You don't need a Dutch oven, baking stone, pizza peel, or even a broiler pan to bake a perfect sandwich loaf. The only thing you need is a simple rectangular loaf pan.

Rectangle loaf baking pans are the perfect tool in which to bake many no-knead bread doughs. Because no-knead doughs tend to be on the wet side, shaping the dough into a perfect loaf can sometimes be challenging.

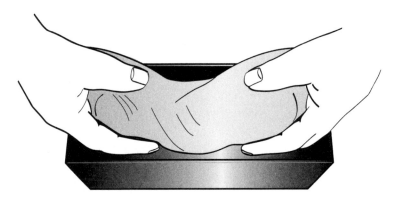

When you've got the dough in a somewhat-loaf shape, all you have to do is put it in the loaf pan and your work is done.

When the dough is baked in a loaf pan, the pan does all the work. It perfectly shapes wet doughs into a consistent rectangle shape that's even from the first slice to the last, making these breads the ideal shape for sandwiches and toast.

Special Techniques

Even though the loaf pan does most of the work doesn't mean loaf breads have to be boring! With a few simple techniques, you can add more interest—and flavor—to your loaf breads.

For example, in the Classic Butter-Split White Sandwich Bread, by making a slash down the center of the loaf before you bake it, you can get that classic sandwich-bread look.

And it's easy to get the swirl in this chapter's Cinnamon-Raisin Swirl Bread. After you've rolled out the dough, simply spread the cinnamon mixture evenly over the surface, sprinkle with raisins, roll up the dough, and drop it in the pan. This works with other ingredients, too, and is an easy way to add some pizzaz to your loaf breads.

To get the swirl in loaf breads, simply roll out the dough, add your swirl ingredients, roll up the dough, and it's ready for the pan.

And to create classic brioche à tête shape, you can use classic fluted brioche tins instead of the standard loaf pan. Place a ball of dough in the tin, press a smaller ball on top, and—ta da!—brioche à tête.

Fluted brioche tins can serve as the loaf pan for brioche à tête. Separate a small piece (about 1/8 of the entire dough) of dough and shape into a ball. After shaping the larger piece into a ball and placing into the mold, place the smaller ball on top.

No Loafing Around

Knowing when a loaf bread is fully baked can be a little tricky. The loaf will have risen and the top will be golden before the center is baked through. There's nothing worse than cutting into your bread to find that it's doughy in the middle!

A thermometer is a huge help because it'll let you know in exactly what state the dough is. Generally, the temperature should fall between 200°F and 205°F. After it hits 212°F, moisture will start evaporating from the loaf and it will begin to dry out. If you don't have a thermometer handy, a long skewer will work in a pinch. Insert it into the center, and if it comes out doughy, the loaf needs more time. When the skewer comes out clean or with just a few moist crumbs, the loaf is ready to come out.

BAKER'S DOZEN

If you don't want to ruin the beautiful top of your loaf with a hole from the thermometer or skewer, take its temperature from the side. With toweled hands, gently hold the pan to the side and pull out the almost-baked loaf just enough to poke the thermometer into the side of the loaf.

When the loaf is out of the oven, leave it in the pan only a few minutes. Quite a bit of moist steam escapes from the loaf when it has finished baking, and if left in the pan for a long time, the pan will trap all the steam, leading to a loaf with a soggy bottom. Cool the loaf only briefly in the pan and then finish on a cooling rack that allows for proper ventilation.

Cinnamon-Raisin Swirl Bread

In this surprising loaf, plump, juicy raisins; brown sugar; and spicy cinnamon spiral into a craggy white bread. It's perfect toasted and buttered the next day.

Yield:	Prep time:	Rest and rise time:	Cook time:	Serving size:
1 (8¹/₂×4¹/₂×3-inch) loaf	15 minutes	6 to 24 hours	50 minutes	1 (¹/₂-inch) slice

3 TB. firmly packed light brown sugar

2 TB. ground cinnamon

3¹/₂ cups all-purpose flour

5 TB. sugar

1³/₄ tsp. yeast

1¹/₂ tsp. salt

1 large egg

1 cup whole milk

¹/₄ cup plus 1 TB. water

5 TB. unsalted butter, melted

¹/₃ cup raisins

1. In a small bowl, combine brown sugar and cinnamon. Cover with plastic wrap and set aside.

2. In a large bowl, stir together flour, sugar, yeast, and salt. Stir in egg, milk, water, and 2 tablespoons melted butter until completely combined. Loosely cover with plastic wrap and let rise at room temperature for about 2 or 3 hours or until dough has doubled in size and surface is covered with large bubbles.

3. Refrigerate for at least 3 hours, or preferably overnight.

4. Preheat the oven to 350°F. Coat a 8¹/₂×4¹/₂×3-inch loaf pan with nonstick cooking spray.

5. On a well-floured work surface and with well-floured hands, roll dough into a 8×10-inch rectangle. Brush dough with 2 tablespoons melted butter, sprinkle brown sugar and cinnamon mixture evenly over top, and follow with raisins.

6. Beginning at the short end, gently roll dough into a cylinder. Pinch ends closed to seal and place cylinder in the pan. Brush the top with remaining 1 tablespoon melted butter and let rest for about 45 minutes.

7. Bake for about 50 minutes or until golden, firm, and a thermometer inserted into the center of loaf registers between 200°F and 205°F.

8. Cool in the pan for 20 minutes. Remove from the pan and cool completely on a cooling rack. Cut into slices and serve.

BAKER'S DOZEN

Because no-knead doughs are slightly wetter than kneaded doughs, you might find that it sticks to your work surface when you try to roll it up into the cylinder. Just keep your hands well floured and use a bench scraper to nudge the dough from the board.

Classic Butter-Split White Sandwich Bread

It won't take long for this slightly sweet, buttery bread with a tender crumb to become a classic in your home.

Yield:	Prep time:	Rest and rise time:	Cook time:	Serving size:
1 (8^1/$_2$×4^1/$_2$×3-inch) loaf	15 minutes	6 to 24 hours	50 minutes	1 (^{1}/$_2$-inch) slice

3^1/$_2$ cups all-purpose flour	1 cup whole milk
3 TB. sugar	^{3}/$_4$ cup lukewarm water
1^1/$_2$ tsp. yeast	3 TB. unsalted butter, melted
1^1/$_2$ tsp. salt	1 TB. vegetable shortening, melted

1. In a large bowl, stir together flour, sugar, yeast, and salt. Stir in milk, water, 1 tablespoon melted butter, and melted shortening until completely combined.

2. Loosely cover with plastic wrap and let rise at room temperature for about 2 or 3 hours or until dough has doubled in size and surface is covered with large bubbles.

3. Refrigerate for at least 3 hours, or preferably overnight.

4. Preheat the oven to 350°F. Coat a 8^1/$_2$×4^1/$_2$×3-inch loaf pan with nonstick cooking spray.

5. On a well-floured work surface and with well-floured hands, shape dough into an oval and place in the pan, seam side down. Let loaf rest for about 30 to 40 minutes to come to room temperature and rise slightly.

6. With a sharp knife, make a long, shallow slash lengthwise down the center of top of loaf. Bake for 20 minutes and then brush top with 1 tablespoon melted butter. Bake for another 20 minutes and brush with remaining 1 tablespoon butter. Continue to bake for about 10 more minutes or until golden, firm, and a thermometer inserted into the center of loaf registers about 200°F.

7. Cool in the pan for 20 minutes. Remove from the pan and cool completely on a cooling rack. Cut into slices and serve.

BAKER'S DOZEN

Keep your bread as fresh as possible by cutting slices from the middle of the loaf first. Pushing the two halves together helps seal in moisture.

Whole-Wheat Sandwich Bread

Whole-wheat flour adds complex, earthy flavor to this soft-textured, slightly sweet bread.

Yield:	Prep time:	Rest and rise time:	Cook time:	Serving size:
1 (8$\frac{1}{2}$x4$\frac{1}{2}$x3-inch) loaf	10 minutes	6 to 24 hours	50 minutes	1 ($\frac{1}{2}$-inch) slice

2$\frac{1}{2}$ cups whole-wheat flour

1 cup bread flour

2 tsp. yeast

1$\frac{1}{4}$ tsp. salt

1 cup plus 1 TB. whole milk

6 TB. lukewarm water

$\frac{1}{4}$ cup honey

1 TB. unsalted butter, melted

1 TB. vegetable shortening, melted

1. In a large bowl, stir together whole-wheat flour, bread flour, yeast, and salt. Stir in 1 cup milk, water, honey, melted butter, and melted shortening until completely combined.

2. Loosely cover with plastic wrap and let rise at room temperature for about 2 or 3 hours or until dough has doubled in size and surface is covered with large bubbles.

3. Refrigerate for at least 3 hours, or preferably overnight.

4. Preheat the oven to 350°F. Coat a 8$\frac{1}{2}$x4$\frac{1}{2}$x3-inch loaf pan with nonstick cooking spray.

5. On a well-floured work surface and with well-floured hands, shape dough into an oval and place in the pan, seam side down. Let loaf rest for about 30 to 40 minutes to come to room temperature and rise slightly.

6. With a sharp knife, make a long, shallow slash lengthwise down the center of top of loaf. Brush with remaining 1 tablespoon milk, and bake for about 50 minutes or until golden, firm, and a thermometer inserted into the center of loaf registers between 200°F and 205°F.

7. Cool in the pan for 20 minutes. Remove from the pan and cool completely on a cooling rack. Cut into slices and serve.

BREAD HEAD

If you'd like to include more whole wheat in your diet but aren't used to the bolder flavor of whole-wheat flour, there's a great new product on the market just for you: *white* whole-wheat flour. Ground from white spring wheat rather than the traditional red wheat, white whole-wheat flour has all the nutrition of whole wheat but with a milder taste.

Honey-Oatmeal Bread

A triple-whammy of oats packs this soft-crusted bread with moist, hearty texture and nutty flavor. Lightly sweetened, it's perfect as sandwich bread or buttered fresh from the oven.

Yield:	Prep time:	Rest and rise time:	Cook time:	Serving size:
1 (8½×4½×3-inch) loaf	1 hour	6 to 24 hours	45 minutes	1 (½-inch) slice

3 TB. steel-cut oats	2 tsp. instant yeast
¼ cup boiling water	1¼ tsp. salt
2½ cups all-purpose flour	⅓ cup honey
½ cup oat flour	2 TB. vegetable oil
½ cup plus 3 TB. *rolled oats*	1¼ cups lukewarm water

1. In a small bowl, stir together steel-cut oats and boiling water. Cool to room temperature.

2. In a large bowl, stir together all-purpose flour, oat flour, ½ cup rolled oats, yeast, and salt. Stir in cooled oat mixture along with honey, vegetable oil, and lukewarm water until completely combined.

3. Loosely cover with plastic wrap and let rise at room temperature for about 2 or 3 hours or until dough has doubled in size and surface is covered with large bubbles.

4. Refrigerate for at least 3 hours, or preferably overnight.

5. Coat a 8½×4½×3-inch loaf pan with nonstick cooking spray. Sprinkle 2 tablespoons rolled oats along the inside of the pan.

6. On a well-floured surface and with well-floured hands, gently shape dough into an oval and place into the prepared pan, seam side down. Brush top of loaf with water and sprinkle remaining 1 tablespoon oats on top. Let rise for 1 hour.

7. About 30 minutes before baking, preheat the oven to 350°F.

8. With a sharp knife, make a long, shallow slash lengthwise down the center of top of loaf. Bake for about 45 minutes or until deep golden brown, firm, and a thermometer inserted into the center of loaf registers about 205°F.

9. Cool in the pan for 20 minutes. Remove from the pan and cool completely on a cooling rack. Cut into slices and serve.

LOAF LINGO

Rolled oats, also known as old-fashioned oats, are highly nutritious and filled with cholesterol-fighting fiber. They're made by passing steamed steel-cut oats through rollers to flatten them.

Brioche

You can't get much more buttery than this bread. Tender and moist, it's the perfect breakfast toast. Go ahead and spread it with butter, I won't tell!

Yield:	Prep time:	Rest and rise time:	Cook time:	Serving size:
1 (8$\frac{1}{2}$x4$\frac{1}{2}$x3-inch) loaf	15 minutes	6 to 24 hours	50 minutes	1 ($\frac{1}{2}$-inch) slice

2$\frac{1}{2}$ cups bread flour

2 TB. sugar

2 tsp. yeast

1$\frac{1}{2}$ tsp. salt

$\frac{1}{2}$ cup lukewarm water

3 large eggs

$\frac{1}{2}$ cup (1 stick) unsalted butter, softened

1 batch Essential Egg Wash (recipe in Chapter 15)

1. In a large bowl, stir together flour, sugar, yeast, salt, and water until completely combined.

2. Loosely cover with plastic wrap and let rise at room temperature for about 2 or 3 hours or until dough has doubled in size and surface is covered with large bubbles.

3. Stir in eggs and softened butter until completely combined. Refrigerate dough for at least 3 hours, or preferably overnight.

4. Preheat the oven to 350°F. Coat a 8$\frac{1}{2}$x4$\frac{1}{2}$x3-inch loaf pan with nonstick cooking spray.

5. On a well-floured work surface and with well-floured hands, gently shape dough into an oval and place in the pan, seam side down. Let rest for about 30 to 40 minutes to come to room temperature and rise.

6. Brush with Essential Egg Wash, and bake for about 50 minutes or until golden, firm, and a thermometer inserted into the center of loaf registers between 200°F and 210°F.

7. Cool in the pan for 20 minutes. Remove from the pan and cool completely on a cooling rack. Cut into slices and serve.

Make it your own: It's easy to create the classic brioche à tête shape with this dough and fluted brioche tins. Simply divide the dough into 1-cup portions and fill individual brioche molds, or divide the dough in half and fill 2 medium-size molds. Place a small round ball of dough in the pan, and press a smaller round piece on top. Baking times will be less for these smaller loaves—approximately 25 to 40 minutes.

DOUGH DON'T

Be sure the butter is nice and soft before adding to this dough or it won't successfully incorporate.

Green's Crunchy Seed Bread

A crunchy assortment of seeds makes this bread explode with texture and nutty flavor. And with it toasted and drizzled with honey, you'll almost forget how healthy it is for you!

Yield:	Prep time:	Rest and rise time:	Cook time:	Serving size:
1 (8^1/$_2$×4^1/$_2$×3-inch) loaf	30 minutes	6 to 24 hours	50 minutes	1 (^{1}/$_2$-inch) slice

1 cup unroasted sunflower seeds

3 TB. flaxseeds

2 TB. sesame seeds

3 TB. poppy seeds

2 TB. millet (optional)

2^1/$_2$ cups all-purpose flour

1 cup whole-wheat flour

2^1/$_4$ tsp. yeast

1^1/$_2$ tsp. salt

1 cup lukewarm water

^{3}/$_4$ cup whole milk

^{1}/$_3$ cup honey

3 TB. vegetable oil

1 batch Essential Egg Wash (recipe in Chapter 15)

1. Place sunflower, flax, sesame, poppy seeds, and millet (if using) in a medium skillet over medium heat and lightly toast for about 2 minutes. Set aside and cool completely. Reserve 2 tablespoons toasted seed mixture for topping.

2. In a large bowl, stir together all-purpose flour, whole-wheat flour, yeast, salt, and seed mixture. Stir in water, milk, honey, and vegetable oil until completely combined.

3. Loosely cover with plastic wrap and let dough rise at room temperature for about 2 or 3 hours or until dough has doubled in size and surface is covered with large bubbles.

4. Refrigerate for at least 3 hours, or preferably overnight.

5. Preheat the oven to 350°F. Coat a 8^1/$_2$×4^1/$_2$×3-inch loaf pan with nonstick cooking spray.

6. On a well-floured work surface and with well-floured hands, shape dough into an oval and place in the pan, seam side down. Let loaf rest for about 30 to 40 minutes to come to room temperature and rise slightly.

7. Brush top of loaf with Essential Egg Wash and sprinkle with reserved 2 tablespoons seeds. Bake for about 50 minutes or until golden, firm, and a thermometer inserted into center of loaf registers about 210°F.

8. Cool in the pan for 20 minutes. Remove from the pan and cool completely on a cooling rack. Cut into slices and serve.

BAKER'S DOZEN

This bread contains an abundance of healthful seeds that, due to their high oil content, can go rancid quickly, making them bitter. Prolong their shelf life by storing them in an airtight container in the refrigerator.

Pimento Pepper Jack Bread

Studded with smoky chunks of roasted red peppers, this bread also gets a bit of kick from the pepper jack cheese.

Yield:	Prep time:	Rest and rise time:	Cook time:	Serving size:
1 (8¹/₂×4¹/₂×3-inch) loaf	20 minutes	6 to 24 hours	50 minutes	1 (¹/₂-inch) slice

2¹/₂ cups all-purpose flour

3 TB. sugar

2 tsp. yeast

1¹/₂ tsp. salt

³/₄ cup milk

¹/₃ cup lukewarm water

2 TB. unsalted butter, melted

1 large egg

1¹/₂ cups pepper jack cheese, shredded

¹/₂ cup *pimentos,* chopped

1. In a large bowl, stir together flour, sugar, yeast, and salt. Stir in milk, water, melted butter, egg, cheese, and pimentos until completely combined.

2. Loosely cover with plastic wrap and let rise at room temperature for about 2 or 3 hours or until dough has doubled in size and surface is covered with large bubbles.

3. Refrigerate for at least 3 hours, or preferably overnight.

4. Preheat the oven to 350°F. Coat a 8¹/₂×4¹/₂×3-inch loaf pan with nonstick cooking spray.

5. On a well-floured work surface and with well-floured hands, shape dough into an oval and place in the pan, seam side down. Let loaf rest for about 30 to 40 minutes to come to room temperature and rise slightly.

6. Bake for about 50 minutes or until golden, firm, and a thermometer inserted into the center of loaf registers between 200°F and 205°F.

7. Cool in the pan for 20 minutes. Remove from the pan and cool completely on a cooling rack. Cut into slices and serve.

LOAF LINGO

A **pimento** is a small, sweet red pepper with a flavor similar to a red bell pepper. It's usually sold in jars, roasted, which gives it a smoky flavor. Jarred roasted red peppers work just as well in this recipe.

Root Beer–Molasses Bread

Reminiscent of a deep, dark Boston brown bread, this loaf is full of molasses flavor. The surprise ingredient, root beer, will keep your guests guessing!

Yield:	Prep time:	Rest and rise time:	Cook time:	Serving size:
1 (8¹/₂×4¹/₂×3-inch) loaf	10 minutes	6 to 24 hours	50 minutes	1 (¹/₂-inch) slice

1¹/₂ cups whole-wheat flour
1¹/₂ cups bread flour
2¹/₄ tsp. yeast
1¹/₄ tsp. salt

1 (12-oz.) bottle root beer (1¹/₂ cups)
²/₃ cup molasses
4 TB. vegetable shortening, melted
3 TB. lukewarm water

1. In a large bowl, stir together whole-wheat flour, bread flour, yeast, and salt. Stir in root beer, molasses, melted shortening, and water until completely combined.

2. Loosely cover with plastic wrap and let rise at room temperature for about 2 or 3 hours or until dough has doubled in size and surface is covered with large bubbles.

3. Refrigerate for at least 3 hours, or preferably overnight.

4. Preheat the oven to 350°F. Coat a 8¹/₂×4¹/₂×3-inch loaf pan with nonstick cooking spray.

5. On a well-floured work surface and with well-floured hands, shape dough into an oval and place in the pan, seam side down. Let loaf rest for about 30 to 40 minutes to come to room temperature and rise slightly.

6. Bake for about 50 minutes or until dark golden brown, firm, and a thermometer inserted into the center of loaf registers between 200°F and 205°F.

7. Cool in the pan for 20 minutes. Remove from the pan and cool completely on a cooling rack. Cut into slices and serve.

BREAD HEAD

So what flavors a root beer? You guessed it, roots! Well, mostly. Depending on the maker, root beer can be flavored with any combination of roots or barks. Sassafras and sarsaparilla are the most widely known, but a host of other plants such as ginger root, birch bark, juniper berries, dandelion root, and cinnamon bark are also used in flavoring root beer.

Flatbreads, Pizzas, and Focaccia

In This Chapter

- Thin flatbreads
- Pizza basics—and then some
- Thick focaccia

The recipes in this chapter demonstrate the sheer versatility of bread. From light and crispy lavash, to thick Sicilian pizza piled with a mountain of toppings, the bread recipes in this chapter fit any type of craving.

These breads span the ages. By baking naan or lavash, you'll be paying homage to some of the earliest forms of bread-making. And the recipes are so simple that I guarantee you'll think twice before buying another package of premade pitas!

And today, you'd be hard pressed to find a more popular bread in this country than pizza dough. And there's good reason why. Pizza is so much more than bread—it's a meal. Out of all the recipes in the book, these are the ones to turn to when you want to put a fast, fresh, complete dinner on the table.

Pizza Rules

Nothing beats a fresh, piping-hot homemade pizza loaded with your favorite toppings. The pizza recipes in this chapter will have you pulling out pizzas from your oven better than those your local pizzeria delivers.

But before you grab your pizza cutter, you need to know a few pizza-specific things:

- Be sure your baking stone is preheated for at least 45 minutes. Pizzas bake fairly quickly, so to get that crisp bottom crust, the stone needs to be super hot.

- When the pizza has been placed on the peel, slide it onto the hot stone fairly quickly. If you leave the dough on the peel for too long, it will begin to soften and stick to the peel, making it difficult to transfer.

- Even if the pizza sticks a little, or doesn't slide onto the baking stone in a perfect circular shape, don't fret. The irregular shape adds to the organic, rustic beauty of a fresh artisan pizza.

- Remember that toppings suggested in the recipes are merely that— suggestions to give you inspiration. A pizza can be anything you want it to be. Let your creative juices run wild!

 DOUGH DON'T

When creating your own pizza, the amount of toppings you add affects the crispiness of the crust. Don't load too many toppings on the dough, or it will be difficult to get a crisp crust.

Naan

This classic Indian flatbread is slightly tangy and gets delicious caramelized spots while under the oven broiler. It's the perfect complement to any Indian-inspired meal.

Yield:	Prep time:	Rest time:	Cook time:	Serving size:
8 (6-inch) naan	10 minutes	6 to 24 hours	3 minutes	1 naan

2½ cups all-purpose flour

1½ tsp. yeast

1 tsp. sugar

1 tsp. salt

⅛ tsp. baking powder

1 cup plus 2 TB. lukewarm water

3 TB. plain yogurt

2 TB. vegetable oil

½ cup (1 stick) unsalted butter

1. In a large bowl, stir together flour, yeast, sugar, salt, and baking powder. Stir in water, yogurt, and vegetable oil until completely combined.

2. Loosely cover with plastic wrap and let rise at room temperature for about 2 or 3 hours or until dough has doubled in size and surface is covered with large bubbles.

3. Refrigerate for at least 3 hours, or preferably overnight.

4. Place a baking stone on the middle oven rack, and preheat the broiler for 15 minutes.

5. In a small saucepan over medium heat, heat butter, gently swirling pan, until butter solids sink to the bottom of the pan. Spoon clear butter from solids and set aside, keeping warm. Discard solids.

6. Place a small bowl of water next to your work surface.

7. On a well-floured work surface and with well-floured hands, divide dough into 8 equal pieces. Roll each piece into a 6-inch disc. (You can roll 2 at a time if you like.)

8. Lightly brush both sides of each naan with water, and place 2 naan at a time onto the baking stone. Broil for about 3 minutes or until naan are puffed and covered with uneven dark brown spots.

9. Using a metal spatula, carefully remove naan, place on a plate, and brush with melted butter. Repeat with remaining naans. Serve warm or at room temperature.

BAKER'S DOZEN

Brushing the naan with water adds moisture to the baking environment and helps keep the naan soft while it bakes. Naan cooks fast, so keep a close watch on it to avoid burning.

Pita Pockets

This delicious bread puffs in the hot oven, forming a hollow pocket to fill with your favorite sandwich filling.

Yield:	Prep time:	Rest time:	Cook time:	Serving size:
8 (6-inch) pitas	10 minutes	6 to 24 hours	10 minutes	1 pita

3 cups bread flour	2 tsp. yeast
4 tsp. sugar	1 cup plus 4 TB. lukewarm water
2¹/₂ tsp. salt	6 TB. olive oil

1. In a medium bowl, stir together flour, sugar, salt, and yeast. Stir in water and olive oil until completely combined.

2. Loosely cover with plastic wrap and let rise at room temperature for about 2 or 3 hours or until dough has doubled in size and surface is covered with large bubbles.

3. Refrigerate for at least 3 hours, or preferably overnight.

4. Place a baking stone on the middle oven rack, and preheat the oven to 500°F.

5. On a well-floured work surface and with well-floured hands, divide dough into 8 pieces. Using a rolling pin, roll each piece into a 6-inch disc.

6. Place 2 pitas at a time onto the baking stone, and bake for about 8 to 10 minutes or until puffed and browned. Transfer pitas to cooling rack. Repeat with remaining pitas.

7. While still warm, poke each pita with a knife to deflate. Serve warm or allow to cool completely.

Make it your own: You can make whole-wheat pitas using 2 cups bread flour and 1 cup whole-wheat flour instead of the bread flour called for here.

BREAD HEAD

On May 19, 2001, on the island of Crete in Greece, Georgios Mavroleon and Nektarios Fintikakis made the world's largest pita bread. It weighed just over 110 pounds.

Crispy Lavash

Light, thin, and crunchy, this flatbread is like a giant cracker. Poppy and sesame seeds give it a nutty, toasted flavor.

Yield:	Prep time:	Rest time:	Cook time:	Serving size:
8 lavash	10 minutes	6 to 24 hours	25 minutes	1 lavash

1³/₄ cups whole-wheat flour	1¹/₃ cups water, lukewarm
1¹/₄ cups bread flour	¹/₂ cup milk
2 tsp. yeast	¹/₄ cup poppy seeds
2 tsp. salt	¹/₄ cup sesame seeds

1. In a large bowl, stir together whole-wheat flour, bread flour, yeast, and salt. Stir in water until completely combined.

2. Loosely cover with plastic wrap and let rise at room temperature for about 2 or 3 hours or until dough has doubled in size and surface is covered with large bubbles.

3. Refrigerate for at least 3 hours, or preferably overnight.

4. Place the oven rack on the upper-middle and lower-middle positions, and preheat the oven to 400°F. Lightly grease 2 baking sheets with vegetable oil.

5. On a well-floured work surface and with well-floured hands, divide dough into 8 equal pieces. Working 1 piece at a time, roll lavash as thin as possible, about 8 inches round and ¹/₁₆-inch thick. Shape may be irregular.

6. Carefully place 2 lavash on each baking sheet. Brush lavash with milk and sprinkle with about 1 tablespoon poppy or sesame seeds.

7. Bake for about 20 to 25 minutes or until lavash is crisp and deep golden brown in spots.

8. Using a bench scraper, remove lavash and place on a wire rack to cool. Let the baking sheet cool before using it for the next batch of lavash.

BAKER'S DOZEN

Rolling the lavash super thin is the secret to its crackerlike texture. Thicker pieces won't be as crispy.

Southwestern Blue Cornmeal Flatbread

Roasted corn, black beans, cilantro, and queso fresco top this hearty but tender flatbread. The blue cornmeal turns the dough a unique purple color.

Yield:	Prep time:	Rest time:	Cook time:	Serving size:
1 (12-inch) flatbread	20 minutes	6 to 24 hours	30 minutes	1 (4-inch) wedge

$^3/_4$ cup bread flour

$^1/_2$ cup *blue cornmeal*

$^1/_2$ tsp. yeast

1 tsp. salt

$^1/_2$ tsp. sugar

$^1/_2$ cup lukewarm water

5 TB. olive oil

$^1/_3$ cup yellow cornmeal

$^1/_2$ cup canned black beans, drained and rinsed

$^1/_2$ cup frozen or canned corn kernels

$^1/_3$ cup *queso fresco*

$^1/_2$ cup chopped fresh cilantro

1. In a large bowl, stir together flour, blue cornmeal, yeast, $^1/_2$ teaspoon salt, and sugar. Add water and 2 tablespoons olive oil, and stir until completely combined.

2. Loosely cover with plastic wrap and let rise at room temperature for about 2 or 3 hours or until dough has doubled in size and surface is covered with large bubbles.

3. Refrigerate for at least 3 hours, or preferably overnight.

4. Place a baking stone on the bottom oven rack, and preheat the oven to 500°F for at least 45 minutes. Sprinkle a pizza peel liberally with cornmeal.

5. On a well-floured work surface, use a rolling pin to roll dough into an 11-inch circle. Immediately transfer dough circle to the pizza peel.

6. Working quickly, drizzle 1 tablespoon olive oil over flatbread and sprinkle evenly with black beans and corn. Drizzle with remaining 2 tablespoons olive oil, and sprinkle with remaining $^1/_2$ teaspoon salt. Quickly slide flatbread onto the baking stone.

7. Bake for about 30 minutes or until flatbread is browned and crispy. Using the pizza peel, remove flatbread and slide onto a cutting board. Drizzle flatbread with queso fresco, and top with cilantro. Cut into slices, and serve hot.

LOAF LINGO

Blue cornmeal is made from blue corn (also called Hopi corn). It's still cultivated in the Southwest by Native Americans. Yellow cornmeal may be substituted if you can't find the blue. **Queso fresco** is a traditional Mexican cheese. It's mild in flavor and slightly salty. When heated, it softens and becomes creamy, but it won't melt.

Arugula and Parmesan Flatbread

Two hits of Parmesan flavor in this thin and crispy flatbread, which is topped with a heap of fresh arugula and lemon vinaigrette.

Yield:	Prep time:	Rest time:	Cook time:	Serving size:
1 (12-inch) flatbread	10 minutes	6 to 24 hours	12 minutes	1 (4-inch) wedge

1 cup all-purpose flour	$^1/_4$ cup grated Parmesan cheese
$^1/_2$ tsp. salt	3 cups fresh arugula
$^1/_2$ tsp. yeast	$^1/_4$ cup chopped walnuts, lightly toasted
$^3/_4$ cup plus 1 TB. lukewarm water	
4 TB. extra-virgin olive oil	$^1/_2$ cup Parmesan cheese shavings
$^1/_3$ cup yellow cornmeal	Kosher salt
1 TB. lemon juice	Freshly ground black pepper

1. In a medium bowl, stir together flour, salt, and yeast. Stir in water and 1 tablespoon olive oil until completely combined.

2. Loosely cover with plastic wrap and let rise at room temperature for about 2 or 3 hours or until dough has doubled in size and surface is covered with large bubbles.

3. Refrigerate for at least 3 hours, or preferably overnight.

4. Place a baking stone on the bottom oven rack, and preheat the oven to 500°F for at least 45 minutes. Sprinkle pizza peel liberally with cornmeal.

5. In a medium bowl, slowly whisk remaining 3 tablespoons olive oil into lemon juice until combined. Set aside.

6. On a well-floured surface and with well-floured hands, roll dough into a thin, 13-inch circle. Place dough circle on the pizza peel. Sprinkle with grated Parmesan cheese, and quickly slide dough circle onto the baking stone.

7. Bake for about 12 minutes or until lightly browned and set. Using the pizza peel, remove flatbread from the oven.

8. In a medium bowl, toss arugula with lemon juice. Spread on top of baked flat-bread. Sprinkle with walnuts and shaved Parmesan, season with kosher salt and black pepper, cut into wedges, and serve.

BREAD HEAD

When choosing Parmesan cheese, pick a high-quality version such as Parmesan Reggiano. It's made from raw cow's milk, can be aged as long as 2 or more years, and has a deep nutty flavor and delicious crunchy crystals.

Everyday Pizza

This is the no-knead pizza recipe you'll return to time after time. It's delicious as prepared, or you can easily customize it with your favorite pizza toppings.

Yield:	Prep time:	Rest time:	Cook time:	Serving size:
1 (13-inch) pizza	20 minutes	6 to 24 hours	20 minutes	1 (4-inch) wedge

1½ cups bread flour

¾ tsp. salt

¾ tsp. yeast

1 cup lukewarm water

2 TB. olive oil

⅓ cup yellow cornmeal

1 batch Quick Pizza Sauce (recipe in Chapter 15)

¼ cup grated Parmesan cheese

1½ cups shredded mozzarella cheese

1. In a medium bowl, stir together flour, salt, and yeast. Stir in water and olive oil until completely combined.

2. Loosely cover with plastic wrap and let rise at room temperature for about 2 or 3 hours or until dough has doubled in size and surface is covered with large bubbles.

3. Refrigerate for at least 3 hours, or preferably overnight.

4. Place a baking stone on the bottom oven rack, and preheat the oven to 500°F for at least 45 minutes. Sprinkle a pizza peel liberally with cornmeal.

5. On a well-floured work surface, use a rolling pin to roll dough into a 13-inch circle. Immediately transfer dough circle to the pizza peel.

6. Working quickly, spread Quick Pizza Sauce over dough, leaving a 1-inch border around the edge. Sprinkle Parmesan and mozzarella cheeses over sauce.

7. Slide pizza onto the baking stone, and bake for about 20 minutes or until cheese is melted and beginning to brown and edges of pizza are light golden.

8. Use the pizza peel to remove pizza from the baking stone. Cut into wedges, and serve hot.

Make it your own: For sausage pizza, remove the casings from 2 or 3 sweet pork sausages. Break into small pieces, and cook in a skillet over medium heat for about 8 minutes or until cooked halfway through. (The sausage will finish cooking when the pizza bakes.) Drain and sprinkle over cheese before baking pizza.

BAKER'S DOZEN

If the bottom of your pizza isn't as crisp as you'd like, try precooking the crust before adding the toppings. Bake the dough circle for 10 minutes on the baking stone and then remove it and add sauce and toppings. Continue to bake for about 8 more minutes or until cheese is melted.

Cheese Lover's White Pizza with Ham

A twist on the white pizza, clouds of ricotta, mozzarella, and Parmesan cheeses top this ham-flavored crust.

Yield:	Prep time:	Rest time:	Cook time:	Serving size:
1 (13-inch) pizza	20 minutes	6 to 24 hours	15 minutes	1 (4-inch) wedge

$1^1/_2$ cups bread flour

$^1/_2$ tsp. salt

$^3/_4$ tsp. yeast

$^1/_2$ cup diced ham strips

1 cup lukewarm water

3 TB. olive oil

$^1/_3$ cup yellow cornmeal

3 cloves garlic, minced

$^1/_2$ cup grated Parmesan cheese

$1^1/_4$ cups shredded mozzarella cheese

$^3/_4$ cup whole-milk ricotta cheese

1 cup fresh basil leaves, loosely packed

1. In a medium bowl, stir together flour, salt, and yeast. Stir in diced ham, water, and 2 tablespoons olive oil until completely combined.

2. Loosely cover with plastic wrap and let rise at room temperature for about 2 or 3 hours or until dough has doubled in size and surface is covered with large bubbles.

3. Refrigerate for at least 3 hours, or preferably overnight.

4. Place a baking stone on the bottom oven rack, and preheat the oven to 500°F for at least 45 minutes. Sprinkle a pizza peel liberally with cornmeal.

5. On a well-floured work surface, use a rolling pin to roll dough into a 13-inch circle. Immediately transfer dough circle to the pizza peel.

6. Working quickly, sprinkle minced garlic over dough. Sprinkle Parmesan cheese over garlic, followed by shredded mozzarella cheese. Spoon $1^1/_2$ tablespoon portions ricotta on top, and drizzle with remaining 1 tablespoon olive oil.

7. Slide pizza onto the baking stone, and bake for about 15 minutes or until cheese is melted and beginning to brown and edges of pizza are light golden.

8. Use the pizza peel to remove pizza from the baking stone. Place basil leaves over top of pizza, cut into wedges, and serve hot.

Make it your own: If you like, you can substitute chopped pepperoni or other cured meat instead.

BAKER'S DOZEN

To get a well-done top on your pizza, turn the oven to broil for a few seconds after the pizza has finished cooking. Pay careful attention so the pizza doesn't burn!

Deep-Dish Pizza

A bowl of buttery crust holds a tasty tomato and cheese filling your family will love.

Yield:	Prep time:	Rest time:	Rise time:	Cook time:	Serving size:
1 (9-inch) pizza	20 minutes	6 to 24 hours	30 minutes	25 minutes	1 (3-inch) wedge

1¼ cups bread flour

¾ tsp. salt

¾ tsp. yeast

½ tsp. baking powder

7 TB. lukewarm water

3 TB. unsalted butter, melted

2 TB. olive oil

1 batch Quick Pizza Sauce (recipe in Chapter 15)

1 cup shredded mozzarella cheese

1. In a medium bowl, stir together flour, salt, yeast, and baking powder. Stir in water and melted butter until completely combined.

2. Loosely cover with plastic wrap and let rise at room temperature for about 2 or 3 hours or until dough has doubled in size and surface is covered with large bubbles.

3. Refrigerate for at least 3 hours, or preferably overnight.

4. Preheat the oven to 425°F for 30 minutes. Coat the bottom of a 9-inch cake pan with olive oil.

5. With well-floured hands, spread dough into the bottom of the pan, pressing dough about 1 inch up the sides.

6. Spread Quick Pizza Sauce over dough, and sprinkle mozzarella cheese over sauce. Let sit at room temperature for 30 minutes.

7. Bake on the bottom oven rack for 10 minutes. Switch pizza to an upper-middle rack, and bake for 10 to 15 more minutes or until cheese is melted and crust is golden brown.

8. Cool slightly in the pan before cutting into wedges and serving.

BREAD HEAD

The origins of deep-dish pizza in America stem from Chicago, where it was first created in the early 1940s.

Sicilian Pan Pizza

Perfect for serving a crowd, this large pan pizza has a soft crust and is topped with a popular combo of peppers, onions, and black olives.

Yield:	Prep time:	Rest time:	Rise time:	Cook time:	Serving size:
1 (12×18-inch) pan pizza	20 minutes	6 to 24 hours	45 minutes	40 minutes	1 (4×4-inch) square

4 cups all-purpose flour

5 tsp. yeast

2¹/₂ tsp. salt

1¹/₂ cups lukewarm water

10 TB. olive oil

1 batch Quick Pizza Sauce (recipe in Chapter 15)

¹/₂ cup grated Parmesan cheese

2 cups shredded mozzarella cheese

1 large green bell pepper, ribs and seeds removed, and sliced thin

1 large onion, sliced thin

1 cup jumbo black olives, sliced

1. In a large bowl, stir together flour, yeast, and salt. Stir in water and 4 tablespoons olive oil until completely combined.

2. Loosely cover with plastic wrap and let rise at room temperature for about 2 or 3 hours or until dough has doubled in size and surface is covered with large bubbles.

3. Refrigerate for at least 3 hours, or preferably overnight.

4. Preheat the oven to 425°F. Spread 3 tablespoons olive oil in the bottom of a 12×18-inch rimmed baking sheet.

5. With floured hands, add dough to pan and spread out to the edges of the pan.

6. Spread Quick Pizza Sauce over dough, leaving a 1-inch border around the edges. Sprinkle Parmesan and shredded mozzarella cheeses over sauce. Sprinkle sliced bell pepper, onion, and olives evenly over cheese. Drizzle with remaining 3 tablespoons oil.

7. Let dough rise for 45 minutes. Bake for about 40 minutes or until crust is golden brown and vegetables are just cooked. Cut into squares, and serve hot.

BREAD HEAD

The word *Sicilian*, also known as *Sfincione* or *Sfinciuni*, means "thick sponge" and is different from regular pizza because the dough gets a second rise. This adds to its lighter but still toothsome texture.

Rosemary Focaccia

Fresh rosemary leaves, olive oil, and kosher salt flavor this chewy and fluffy aromatic bread. This focaccia is perfect for dipping in extra-virgin olive oil or cutting into squares for sandwiches.

Yield:	Prep time:	Rest time:	Rise time:	Cook time:	Serving size:
1 (12×18-inch) focaccia	10 minutes	6 to 24 hours	60 minutes	30 minutes	1 (3×3-inch) square

4 cups plus 2 TB. bread flour

1¼ cups all-purpose flour

½ cup chopped fresh rosemary leaves

2¾ tsp. yeast

2½ tsp. salt

2¾ cups lukewarm water

10 TB. olive oil

2 tsp. kosher salt

1. In a large bowl, stir together bread flour, all-purpose flour, rosemary, yeast, and salt. Stir in water and 3 tablespoons olive oil until completely combined.

2. Loosely cover with plastic wrap and let rise at room temperature for about 2 or 3 hours or until dough has doubled in size and surface is covered with large bubbles.

3. Refrigerate for at least 3 hours, or preferably overnight.

4. Preheat the oven to 425°F. Coat the bottom of a 12×18-inch rimmed baking sheet with 3 tablespoons olive oil.

5. With well-floured hands, spread dough to the edges of the baking sheet. Spread remaining 4 tablespoons olive oil over dough and press fingertips into dough to make dimples. Sprinkle kosher salt over dough.

6. Let dough rise for about 1 hour or until it reaches the top of the pan. Bake for about 30 minutes or until golden brown. Cool focaccia in the pan, cut into squares, and serve.

BREAD HEAD

In ancient Greece, students would weave rosemary into their hair because it was thought that rosemary aided memory and brain functioning.

Caramelized Onion and Thyme Focaccia

Sweet caramelized onion and cured black olives dress up this thyme-scented focaccia.

Yield:	Prep time:	Rest time:	Rise time:	Cook time:	Serving size:
1 (12×18-inch) focaccia	10 minutes	6 to 24 hours	60 minutes	30 minutes	1 (3×3-inch) square

3 medium onions, halved and sliced into $1/4$-inch slices

11 TB. olive oil

4 cups plus 2 TB. bread flour

$1^1/4$ cups all-purpose flour

2 TB. chopped fresh thyme leaves

$2^3/4$ tsp. yeast

$2^1/2$ tsp. salt

$2^3/4$ cups lukewarm water

$1/2$ cup cured black olives, halved

1. In a medium saucepan over medium heat, add onions and 3 tablespoons oil and cook for 15 to 25 minutes or until onions have cooked down and are golden in color. Cool and then refrigerate until focaccia is ready to be baked.

2. In a large bowl, stir together bread flour, all-purpose flour, thyme, yeast, and salt. Stir in water and 3 tablespoons olive oil until completely combined.

3. Loosely cover with plastic wrap and let rise at room temperature for about 2 or 3 hours or until dough has doubled in size and surface is covered with large bubbles.

4. Refrigerate for at least 3 hours, or preferably overnight.

5. Preheat the oven to 425°F. Coat the bottom of a 12×18-inch rimmed baking sheet with 3 tablespoons olive oil.

6. With floured hands, spread dough to the edges of the baking sheet. Spread caramelized onions over dough. Press olives into onions. Drizzle remaining 2 tablespoons olive oil over focaccia.

7. Let dough rise for about 1 hour or until it reaches the top of the pan. Bake for 30 minutes or until golden brown. Cool focaccia in pan, cut into squares, and serve.

BREAD HEAD

Caramelization is the oxidation of sugar in foods when heat is applied. Brown color develops and volatile compounds are released, which produces a distinctive caramel flavor.

Rolls, Bagels, and Other Small Breads

In This Chapter

- Shaping rolls
- Breads you boil
- Rolls, buns, and other doughy snacks

Smaller, individual breads are something to treasure. Quaint and individually sized, these breads make you feel special—and you don't have to share!

Smaller breads are also great for determining portion sizes. It might be difficult to figure out how many loaves to make for 12 people, but individually sized rolls remove all the guesswork.

On a Roll

Rolls are perfect for adding variety and filling the bread basket. And they're pretty easy to bake at home.

Commercial bakeries have machines that divide and shape dough into perfect individual rolls, but shaping by hand is entirely within your reach at home. Forming perfect round rolls may feel awkward when you first begin, but once you get the motion down, it's a total snap. Here's how:

1. After dividing the dough into individual pieces, cup your hand over a portion of dough.

 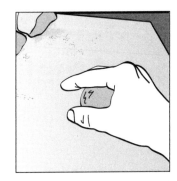

2. Gently press it into the work surface, and move your hand around in a circular motion until dough takes on a round, smooth shape.

After you get accustomed to the feel of it, using both hands will make even quicker work of shaping rolls. The secret is to keep your work surface dusted with just enough flour so that as you roll your rolls, the dough doesn't stick to the surface but also doesn't slide around.

Boiling Before Baking

Bagels are unique because they're one of the few types of bread that are precooked in simmering water before they're baked. Don't skip this step because it contributes to the bagel's trademark chewiness. Do be sure to have your oven preheated and all your tools and equipment in order before you start.

When shaping the bagels before boiling, be sure to only shape two or three bagels to boil at a time. If you shape all the bagels ahead of time, they'll soften too much and be too difficult to work with.

And even though it may seem like there's plenty of water in the pot to boil a bunch, stick with just boiling two or three as recommended in the recipe. Trying to boil more crowds the pot and lowers the water temperature, which can cause uneven cooking.

DOUGH DON'T

Take care when both dropping the bagel into the simmering water and also removing it. You don't want to be splattered with the hot water.

When you drop the bagel in the water, it should first sink to the bottom but then it will rise back up to the surface. If the bagel doesn't rise to the surface after about 30 seconds, it got stuck on the bottom. Gently prod it with a spoon or spatula to release it.

The Twist and Knot

This technique creates a fun, pretzellike variation to the classic round roll. Although it's used in this chapter's Garlicky Pizza Dough Knots, you can incorporate this technique into other rolls.

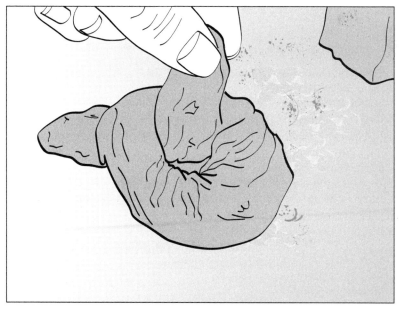

Roll each piece of dough into a rope. Overlap one end of the rope over the other, and pull the end through the loop, forming a knot.

Soft Dinner Rolls

With just the right balance of sweet buttery flavor, these golden, moist rolls are nothing short of addicting.

Yield:	Prep time:	Rest time:	Rise time:	Cook time:	Serving size:
12 rolls	10 minutes	6 to 24 hours	30 minutes	30 minutes	1 roll

1¹/₂ cups all-purpose flour

1¹/₂ cups bread flour

¹/₃ cup sugar

2¹/₂ tsp. yeast

1¹/₂ tsp. salt

¹/₂ cup plus 2 TB. lukewarm whole milk

¹/₂ cup lukewarm water

6 TB. unsalted butter, melted

1 large egg

1 batch Essential Egg Wash (recipe in Chapter 15)

1. In a large bowl, stir together all-purpose flour, bread flour, sugar, yeast, and salt. Stir in milk, water, melted butter, and egg until completely combined.

2. Loosely cover with plastic wrap or a towel and let rise at room temperature for about 2 or 3 hours or until dough has doubled in size and surface is covered with large bubbles.

3. Refrigerate for at least 3 hours, or preferably overnight.

4. Preheat the oven to 350°F. Line a baking sheet with parchment paper.

5. On a lightly floured surface, divide dough into 12 equal portions. Cup your hand over each piece of dough, and roll it into a ball. Place balls on the baking sheet, equally spaced about 1 inch apart. Brush rolls with Essential Egg Wash, and let sit for 30 minutes.

6. Brush rolls a second time with Essential Egg Wash, and bake for 25 to 30 minutes or until rolls are a deep golden brown. Serve rolls warm, or transfer to a cooling rack to cool completely.

Make it your own: Add ¹/₄ cup chopped fresh dill to the dough in step 1.

BAKER'S DOZEN

Spacing the rolls about 1 inch apart keeps them close enough so they bake into each other. This creates soft rolls you can pull apart from each other. Yum.

Petit Pains

Break through this bread's hard and crusty exterior to find a soft and chewy interior, perfect for absorbing a pat of soft butter or for sopping up a rich and meaty soup.

Yield:	Prep time:	Rest time:	Rise time:	Cook time:	Serving size:
12 rolls	10 minutes	6 to 24 hours	15 minutes	30 minutes	1 roll

3 cups bread flour

2 tsp. yeast

1¹/₂ tsp. salt

1¹/₃ cups plus 2 TB. lukewarm water

1 cup hot water

1. In a large bowl, stir together flour, yeast, and salt. Stir in lukewarm water until completely combined.

2. Loosely cover with plastic wrap or a towel and let rise at room temperature for about 2 or 3 hours or until dough has doubled in size and surface is covered with large bubbles.

3. Refrigerate for at least 3 hours, or preferably overnight.

4. Place a broiler tray on the bottom oven rack, and place another rack in the middle position. Preheat the oven to 425°F. Line a baking sheet with parchment paper.

5. On a floured surface, divide dough into 12 equal pieces. Roll each petit pain into a disc. Gently pat disc, slightly flattening it. Fold disc in ¹/₂ and place your hands on either side of petit pain. Gently roll petit pain, tapering ends so roll resembles an elongated football shape about 4 inches long. Place on prepared pan, and repeat with remaining pieces of dough.

6. Let sit at room temperature for 15 minutes. Pour hot water into the broiler tray, and close the oven door for 5 minutes.

7. With a sharp knife or scissors, make a slash down the length of each petit pain. Bake for 25 to 30 minutes or until just pale golden brown. Serve warm.

BREAD HEAD

Pronounced *puh-tee PAN* (not *pain* like pain in the neck!), this French term simply means "bread roll." These rolls freeze especially well.

Crumpets

These individual breakfast breads are cooked in a skillet and resemble an English muffin. Baking powder helps make the texture light and fluffy. Crumpets are full of craggy holes to hold butter and jam.

Yield:	Prep time:	Rest time:	Cook time:	Serving size:
8 crumpets	10 minutes	6 to 24 hours	6 minutes	1 crumpet

2 cups all-purpose flour

$^1/_4$ cup powdered milk

2 tsp. yeast

1 tsp. salt

$^1/_2$ tsp. baking powder

$^3/_4$ cup plus 2 TB. lukewarm water

1 large egg white

$^1/_2$ cup vegetable oil

1. In a medium bowl, stir together flour, powdered milk, yeast, salt, and baking powder. Stir in water until completely combined.

2. Loosely cover with plastic wrap or a towel and let rise at room temperature for about 2 or 3 hours or until dough has doubled in size and surface is covered with large bubbles.

3. Refrigerate for at least 3 hours, or preferably overnight.

4. In a medium bowl, whisk egg white to soft peak. Fold beaten white into dough.

5. Heat 2 teaspoons vegetable oil in a small skillet or griddle over medium heat for 1 minute. Spray a 3- or 4-inch ring mold with nonstick cooking spray. Place ring in skillet, and fill $^1/_2$ full with crumpet dough.

6. Cook for about 3 minutes or until crumpet rises, bubbles appear on top, and bottom is golden brown and set. Using tongs and a small spoon, gently push crumpet from ring mold, and flip crumpet over. Cook for 2 or 3 more minutes.

7. Repeat with remaining dough, adding more oil to the pan as needed. Serve crumpets warm or toasted.

BAKER'S DOZEN

If you don't own a ring mold or cookie cutter with deep sides, a clean tuna can will work in a pinch. Use a can opener to remove both the top and bottom of the can. Just be mindful of any sharp edges.

Hearty Hamburger Buns

Large and soft, these buns are the right complement to a meaty burger or sandwich. The small craggy holes are great for holding ketchup or sandwich spreads.

Yield:	Prep time:	Rest time:	Rise time:	Cook time:	Serving size:
10 buns	15 minutes	6 to 24 hours	30 minutes	20 minutes	1 bun

2 cups bread flour

2 cups all-purpose flour

2 TB. sugar

3 tsp. yeast

1½ tsp. salt

1¾ cups lukewarm milk

4 TB. unsalted butter, melted

3 TB. lukewarm water

1 large egg, slightly beaten

3 TB. sesame seeds

1. In a large bowl, stir together bread flour, all-purpose flour, sugar, yeast, and salt. Stir in milk, melted butter, and water until completely combined.

2. Loosely cover with plastic wrap or a towel and let rise at room temperature for about 2 or 3 hours or until dough has doubled in size and surface is covered with large bubbles.

3. Refrigerate for at least 3 hours, or preferably overnight.

4. Preheat the oven to 400°F for 30 minutes. Line a baking sheet with parchment paper.

5. On a well-floured work surface, divide dough into 10 equal portions. Roll each piece into a ball and gently flatten each ball into a 3½-inch disc. Place on the prepared baking sheet, brush with egg, and let sit for 30 minutes.

6. Gently brush with any remaining egg, sprinkle with sesame seeds, and bake for about 20 minutes or until golden brown.

7. Remove buns from the pan, and place on a cooling rack to cool completely before serving.

BREAD HEAD

The hamburger bun was invented by Walter Anderson in 1916. He later co-founded the White Castle hamburger chain in 1921.

Bagels

These flavorful and chewy homemade bagels get their unique texture from a brief stint in simmering water. The barley malt syrup adds flavor and helps the bagels bake to a light golden brown. When it comes to toppings, the sky's the limit!

Yield:	Prep time:	Rest time:	Cook time:	Serving size:
12 bagels	10 minutes	6 to 24 hours	4 minutes in boiling water, 25 minutes in oven	1 bagel

4 cups bread flour

3 TB. sugar

1 TB. yeast

$2^1/_2$ tsp. salt

$1^1/_2$ cups plus 3 TB. lukewarm water

8 cups tap water for boiling bagels

3 TB. barley malt syrup

1 batch Essential Egg Wash (recipe in Chapter 15)

2 TB. poppy seeds (optional)

2 TB. sesame seeds (optional)

$^1/_3$ cup jarred chopped garlic in oil (optional)

1. In a large bowl, stir together flour, sugar, yeast, and salt. Stir in lukewarm water until completely combined.

2. Loosely cover with plastic wrap or a towel and let rise at room temperature for about 2 or 3 hours or until dough has doubled in size and surface is covered with large bubbles.

3. Refrigerate for at least 3 hours, or preferably overnight.

4. Preheat the oven to 425°F. Line a baking sheet with parchment paper. Line a second baking sheet with paper towels.

5. In a large pot over high heat, stir together tap water and barley malt syrup, and bring to a simmer.

6. Divide dough into 12 equal pieces. Working 2 or 3 pieces at a time, roll each piece into a 6-inch rope and form a circle. Pinch ends closed.

7. Drop bagels into simmering water, and cook for about 2 minutes per side. Adjust heat to keep water at a simmer. Remove bagels from water, and place on paper towel–lined tray to drain. Repeat with remaining bagels.

8. Transfer bagels to the parchment paper–lined baking sheet, and brush with Essential Egg Wash. Sprinkle poppy or sesame seeds on bagels. If using garlic, press garlic onto both top and bottom of bagels.

9. Bake for about 25 minutes or until bagels are golden brown and set. Allow to cool on the pan before serving.

BREAD HEAD

Barley malt syrup is a sweetener made from barley grains. Its addition to the simmering water gives the bagels flavor and helps them brown in the oven. You can swap out the barley syrup for sugar, but it won't have as much depth of flavor.

Onion Bialys

Chewy and dimpled with an onion filling in the center, a bialy is the lazy man's bagel because it's not boiled before it's baked.

Yield:	Prep time:	Rest time:	Rise time:	Cook time:	Serving size:
8 bialys	20 minutes	6 to 24 hours	20 minutes	20 minutes	1 bialy

3 cups bread flour	1 medium onion, minced
2 tsp. sugar	2 TB. olive oil
2 tsp. yeast	1 TB. coarse kosher salt
1³/₄ tsp. salt	
1¹/₂ cups lukewarm water	

1. In a large bowl, stir together flour, sugar, yeast, and salt. Stir in water until completely combined.

2. Loosely cover with plastic wrap or a towel and let rise at room temperature for about 2 or 3 hours or until dough has doubled in size and surface is covered with large bubbles.

3. Refrigerate for at least 3 hours, or preferably overnight.

4. Place the oven racks in the upper-middle and lower-middle positions. Preheat the oven to 425°F. Line 2 baking sheets with parchment paper.

5. In a small bowl, stir together minced onion and olive oil.

6. On a well-floured surface and with well-floured hands, divide dough into 8 pieces. Shape each piece into 4-inch disc. Place 4 discs on each prepared pan. Let sit for 10 minutes.

7. Using your fingertips, press into the center of dough to make an indentation, leaving a 1-inch lip around the border of each bialy.

8. Divide onion mixture among bialys, and gently press in the center. Lightly sprinkle with kosher salt, and let rise for about 10 minutes.

9. Bake for 15 to 20 minutes, rotating the pans halfway through baking, or until bialys are set and a very pale golden brown. Serve warm.

 BAKER'S DOZEN

The bottom of a glass makes easy work of making the indentation in the center of the bialy. Just lightly dip it in flour first and then gently press it into the bialy. And be careful not to overbake the bialy. It's supposed to be on the pale side. Trying to bake it until it's a rich golden brown will dry it out.

Garlicky Pizza Dough Knots

These bite-size treats are studded with bits of garlic and fresh herbs. A double brushing with garlic oil makes them pop with flavor.

Yield:	Prep time:	Rest time:	Cook time:	Serving size:
12 knots	15 minutes	6 to 24 hours	20 minutes	2 knots

1½ cups bread flour

1 TB. chopped fresh basil

1 TB. chopped fresh parsley

6 cloves garlic, minced

¾ tsp. salt

¾ tsp. yeast

1 cup lukewarm water

⅓ cup plus 1 TB. olive oil

1. In a large bowl, stir together flour, basil, parsley, 3 cloves garlic, salt, and yeast. Stir in water and 1 tablespoon olive oil until completely combined.

2. Loosely cover with plastic wrap or a towel and let rise at room temperature for about 2 or 3 hours or until dough has doubled in size and surface is covered with large bubbles.

3. Refrigerate for at least 3 hours, or preferably overnight.

4. Preheat the oven to 475°F. Line a baking sheet with parchment paper.

5. In a small saucepan over medium heat, add remaining ⅓ cup olive oil and remaining 3 cloves garlic, and cook for about 5 minutes or until garlic is translucent.

6. Divide dough into 12 equal pieces. Roll each piece into a 4-inch-long rope and loop into a knot.

7. Place knots on the prepared pan, and bake for about 10 minutes or until just beginning to brown.

8. Brush knots with garlic oil and bake for 10 more minutes or until golden brown. Brush knots a second time with garlic oil, and serve warm.

BAKER'S DOZEN

Unless you want to slay a vampire, you probably don't want any lingering garlic odor on your hands! Try rubbing your hands with salt and baking soda, or lemon juice, after washing.

Breakfast and Holiday Breads

What could make an already-delicious bread even more tasty? Sweeten it, of course! The tempting breads in Part 3 represent the most decadent and over-the-top breads of the recipes in this book. Enriched with sugar, eggs, and butter, they are absolute luxury to eat. When you want to bake something a little extra special, these breads satisfy your sweet tooth like no other.

Nothing wakes up your family faster for breakfast than the sweet, warm smell of sticky buns wafting through the house. And during the holidays, I can never resist the urge to bake batches of breads filled with flavorful dried fruit and crunchy nuts. My recipes for panettone, babka, and stollen will easily become part of your holiday repertoire.

In Part 3, I introduce a technique called lamination to create flaky croissants and buttery Danish. And your friends and family will be mighty impressed when you present to them a challah loaf you've braided yourself.

Sweeter Breads

In This Chapter

- How to laminate dough
- Danish, sticky buns, and other bakery favorites
- Tempting croissants and coffee cakes

Sweet breads, especially breakfast breads, are one of the main reasons bakeries always smell so yummy. One of my first jobs was at a bakery, and I couldn't wait to get to work and smell the aroma of fresh-baked Danish and cinnamon rolls as I opened the door each morning. You, too, will relish the delicious aromas wafting through your kitchen with these wonderful breakfast breads.

The no-knead process makes it easy to have fresh-baked breakfast breads in the morning because you can mix and then rest the dough in the refrigerator overnight. And for breads that are laminated with butter, the process can even be spread out into small steps over a 3-day period.

Laminating Dough

Lamination is the secret to the flaky, buttery layers in breads such as Danish and croissants. Rather than blending the butter into the dough, the lamination method creates alternating layers of butter and dough. Butter contains water. So when the layers of dough and water bake in the oven, the heat turns the water into steam. The steam then expands and puffs the dough into flaky layers.

Laminating a dough successfully can be challenging, but the results are well worth the effort.

Turning the Dough

To get these layers into the dough, the dough goes through a process known as "turning the dough." This is a series of folding and rolling the dough a total of three times. For no-knead doughs, you do this after the dough has finished its rest in the refrigerator.

To begin laminating, you roll out the chilled dough and then spread a lightly chilled mixture of butter and flour on top of the dough. Ideally, the butter and dough will be approximately the same temperature and texture. If the butter is too soft, it will simply blend into the dough and won't create layers. If the butter is too cold and hard, it can break up into tiny bits and can tear the dough. Be sure to allow cold butter to warm to room temperature before placing it on the dough.

After you've spread the butter on the dough, fold the dough over the butter to encase it. Then you roll out the dough and fold it again. This is the dough's first turn. Then you refrigerate the dough briefly (not more than 20 minutes) to allow the gluten to *relax* and keep the butter from getting too warm before you repeat this dough-turning process two more times.

> **LOAF LINGO**
>
> When shaping and handling a dough, the gluten begins to tighten up and can make the dough difficult to roll out. **Relaxing** a dough lets the dough rest briefly after you've worked with it. This short rest enables the gluten to loosen up.

It's important to remember that artisan baking is meant to be fun. Even if your dough tears a little, or if it doesn't bake up with perfect flaky layers, the end result still tastes delicious!

Caring for the Dough

Because laminated doughs are full of butter, keep them as cool as possible prior to shaping. If they sit out for too long, the butter will soften and the dough will be hard to work with.

After shaping but before baking, keep the dough away from extreme heat. The heat causes the butter in the layers to melt, compromising the texture of the finished product.

Shaping the Dough

Enriched doughs are generally a dream to work with because they are soft and pliable. Here's how we shape some of the more intricate breads in this chapter:

After placing filling along the length of the kringle, pull the dough over the filling and press the edges to seal.

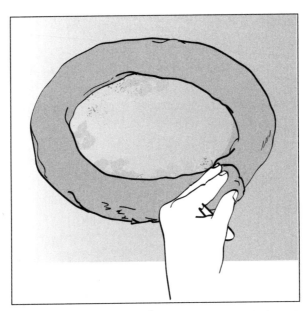

With the seam side down, form an oval with the kringle tube by bringing the ends together, slightly overlapping, and pressing to seal.

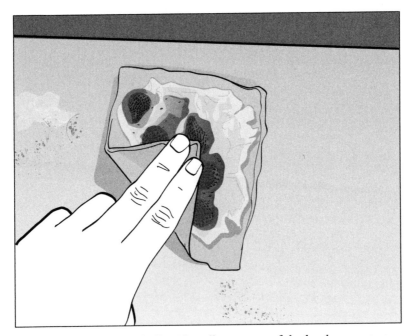

After placing the filling on the Danish, pull one corner of the dough square to the center.

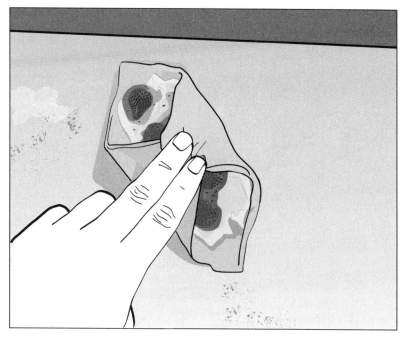

Pull the opposite corner over the filling to slightly overlap, and press to seal.

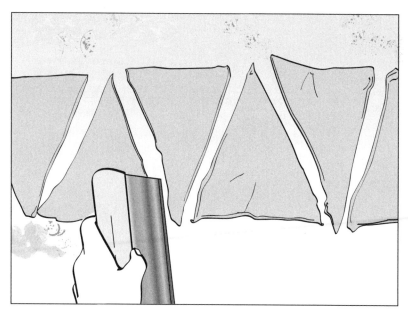

With a bench scraper or a sharp knife, cut the dough into triangles.

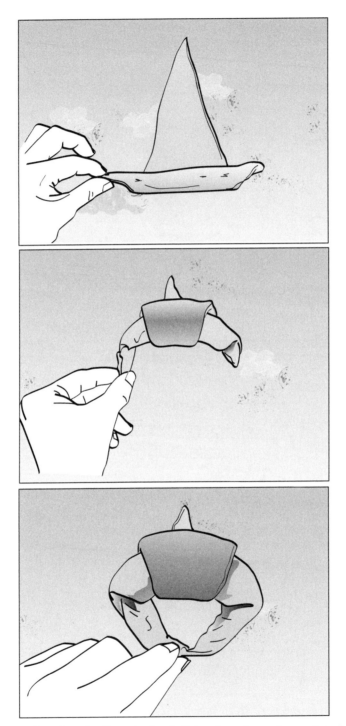

Starting at the wide end, roll up the dough. Bring the ends together, and pinch to seal.

Cinnamon-Streusel Babka

This classic Jewish coffee cake has a cinnamon-swirl filling and a buttery streusel top.

Yield:	Prep time:	Rest time:	Rise time:	Cook time:	Serving size:
1 (10-inch-round) babka	30 minutes	6 to 24 hours	30 minutes	45 minutes	1 (2-inch) slice

3½ cups bread flour

1 cup sugar

1 TB. yeast

1¾ tsp. salt

1 tsp. ground cardamom

1 cup whole milk, lukewarm

3 large egg yolks

2 large eggs

½ cup (1 stick) plus 6 TB. unsalted butter, melted

2 TB. cinnamon

1 batch Essential Egg Wash (recipe in Chapter 15)

1 batch Double-Crumb Streusel (recipe in Chapter 15)

1. In a large bowl, stir together flour, ½ cup sugar, yeast, salt, and cardamom. Stir in milk, egg yolks, eggs, and 6 tablespoons melted butter until completely combined.

2. Loosely cover with plastic wrap or a towel and let rise at room temperature for about 2 or 3 hours or until dough has doubled in size and surface is covered with large bubbles.

3. Refrigerate for at least 3 hours, or preferably overnight.

4. Preheat the oven to 375°F. Spray a 10-inch tube pan with nonstick cooking spray.

5. In a small bowl, stir together remaining ½ cup melted butter, cinnamon, and remaining ½ cup sugar until smooth.

6. On a well-floured work surface and with well-floured hands, roll babka dough into an 18×12-inch rectangle. Spread cinnamon butter evenly over dough.

7. Starting at the long end, gently roll up babka into a cylinder. Use a bench scraper to release dough if it sticks to the work surface.

8. Place cylinder in the prepared pan, overlapping the ends to seal. Brush top with Essential Egg Wash, and sprinkle evenly with Double-Crumb Streusel. Let rest at room temperature for 30 minutes.

9. Bake for 40 to 45 minutes or until babka is golden brown and set and an instant-read thermometer inserted into the center registers about 195°F to 200°F.

10. Cool in the pan for 45 minutes and then remove babka from the pan and place on a wire rack to cool completely. Cut into slices, and serve.

BREAD HEAD

Ground cardamom spice is a popular flavoring for coffee cakes and Danish. However, much of the world's cardamom is used in Arabic countries to flavor their coffee.

Chocolate-Filled Babka

A rich swirl of cinnamon chocolate flavors this classic Jewish coffee cake.

Yield:	Prep time:	Rest time:	Rise time:	Cook time:	Serving size:
1 (10-inch-round) babka	30 minutes	6 to 24 hours	30 minutes	45 minutes	1 (2-inch) slice

3½ cups bread flour	½ tsp. vanilla extract
1 cup sugar	3 oz. semisweet chocolate, finely chopped
1 TB. yeast	
1¾ tsp. salt	1 TB. all-purpose flour
1 tsp. cardamom	1 TB. cocoa powder
1 cup whole milk, lukewarm	1½ tsp. cinnamon
6 TB. unsalted butter, melted	5 TB. unsalted butter, very soft
3 large egg yolks	1 batch Essential Egg Wash (recipe in Chapter 15)
2 large eggs	

1. In a large bowl, stir together flour, ½ cup sugar, yeast, salt, and cardamom. Stir in milk, melted butter, egg yolks, eggs, and vanilla extract until completely combined.

2. Loosely cover with plastic wrap or a towel and let rise at room temperature for about 2 or 3 hours or until dough has doubled in size and surface is covered with large bubbles.

3. Refrigerate for at least 3 hours, or preferably overnight.

4. Preheat the oven to 375°F. Spray a 10-inch tube pan with nonstick cooking spray.

5. In a small bowl, stir together remaining ½ cup sugar, chocolate, all-purpose flour, cocoa powder, and cinnamon until combined.

6. On a well-floured work surface and with well-floured hands, roll babka dough into an 18×12-inch rectangle. Spread softened butter evenly over dough. Sprinkle chocolate mixture evenly over buttered dough.

7. Starting with the long end, gently roll up babka into a cylinder. Use a bench scraper to release dough if it sticks to the work surface.

8. Place cylinder in the prepared pan, overlapping the ends to seal. Brush top with Essential Egg Wash. Let rest at room temperature for 30 minutes.

9. Bake for about 40 to 45 minutes or until babka is golden brown and set and an instant-read thermometer inserted into the center registers about 195°F to 200°F.

10. Cool in the pan for 45 minutes and then remove babka from the pan and place on a wire rack to cool completely. Cut into slices, and serve.

BAKER'S DOZEN

The easiest way to spread softened butter over dough is with an offset spatula. The back of a soup spoon works, too.

Kringle

The delicate dough of this ring-shape Danish coffee cake is filled with a buttery, brown sugar and nut filling.

Yield:	Prep time:	Rest time:	Rise time:	Cook time:	Serving size:
1 (10-inch) ring	30 minutes	6 to 24 hours	30 minutes	30 minutes	1 (2-inch) piece

1 cup all-purpose flour

1 TB. sugar

1¼ tsp. yeast

¼ tsp. salt

¼ cup whole milk, lukewarm

4 TB. unsalted butter, melted

1 large egg yolk

¼ tsp. vanilla extract

¾ cup plus 2 TB. chopped pecans

½ cup firmly packed dark brown sugar

3 TB. unsalted butter, softened

1 batch Essential Egg Wash (recipe in Chapter 15)

1. In a medium bowl, stir together flour, sugar, yeast, and salt. Stir in milk, melted butter, egg yolk, and vanilla extract until completely combined.

2. Loosely cover with plastic wrap or a towel and let rise at room temperature for about 2 or 3 hours or until dough has doubled in size and surface is covered with large bubbles.

3. Refrigerate for at least 3 hours, or preferably overnight.

4. Preheat the oven to 350°F. Line a baking sheet with parchment paper.

5. In a medium bowl, stir together ¾ cup pecans, brown sugar, and softened butter.

6. On a floured work surface and with well-floured hands, roll out dough into a 5×15-inch rectangle. Distribute nut filling along center length of dough. Starting with one end, pull dough around filling and pinch well to seal.

7. Place dough roll, seam side down, onto the prepared baking sheet and form into a ring. Overlap the ends slightly and pinch to seal.

8. Brush ring with Essential Egg Wash, and sprinkle with remaining 2 tablespoons pecans. Let sit for 30 minutes.

9. Bake for about 25 to 30 minutes or until kringle is deep golden brown. Let cool completely on the pan and then transfer to a serving plate and serve.

DOUGH DON'T

This kringle has a delicate dough. Try to avoid cracks when handling after rolling with the filling or the filling may seep out during baking. If you notice a crack or two, pinch the cracks in the dough to seal them before baking.

Pecan Sticky Buns

The king of sweet breakfast pastries, these buttery buns have a ton of pecans, intense cinnamon flavor, and a sweet and sticky glaze.

Yield:	Prep time:	Rest time:	Rise time:	Cook time:	Serving size:
6 sticky buns	30 minutes	6 to 24 hours	20 minutes	30 minutes	1 bun

1¼ cups all-purpose flour

1 cup bread flour

½ cup plus 3 TB. sugar

2 tsp. yeast

1½ tsp. salt

¾ cup plus 2 TB. whole milk

1 large egg

2 TB. vegetable oil

½ cup (1 stick) plus 6 TB. unsalted butter, melted

½ cup firmly packed light brown sugar

1 cup pecan pieces

1 TB. ground cinnamon

1. In a large bowl, stir together all-purpose flour, bread flour, 3 tablespoons sugar, yeast, and salt. Stir in milk, egg, and vegetable oil until completely combined.

2. Loosely cover with plastic wrap or a towel and let rise at room temperature for about 2 or 3 hours or until dough has doubled in size and surface is covered with large bubbles.

3. Refrigerate for at least 3 hours, or preferably overnight.

4. Preheat the oven to 375°F. Spray a 9-inch-round cake pan with nonstick cooking spray. Spread 6 tablespoons melted butter in the cake pan, and sprinkle with brown sugar and ⅓ cup pecans.

5. In a small bowl, stir together remaining ½ cup (1 stick) melted butter, remaining ½ cup sugar, and cinnamon until smooth.

6. On a well-floured work surface and with well-floured hands, roll sticky bun dough into a 14×8-inch rectangle. Spread cinnamon mixture and remaining ⅔ cup pecans evenly over dough.

7. Starting with the long end, gently roll up dough into a cylinder. Use a bench scraper to release dough if it sticks to the work surface. Divide cylinder into 6 pieces.

8. Place 1 roll in the center of the prepared pan and add the remainder in a ring around center roll. Let rolls rest at room temperature for 20 minutes.

9. Bake for about 30 minutes or until rolls are golden brown and set. Cool buns in the pan for 5 minutes.

10. Place a serving plate over the top of the pan, and flip the cake pan over to release sticky buns onto the plate. Serve warm.

Make it your own: For cinnamon buns, omit the mixture that's placed in the bottom of the pan. After the rolls are baked, drizzle with Vanilla Glaze (recipe in Chapter 15).

BAKER'S DOZEN

For smaller, individual buns, you can bake the sticky buns in a muffin tin. Simply divide dough into 12 portions.

Super-Crumb Coffee Cake

Crumb lovers will delight in these crunchy nuggets of buttery crumb streusel atop a lightly sweetened yeast cake.

Yield:	Prep time:	Rest time:	Rise time:	Cook time:	Serving size:
1 (9-inch-round) coffee cake	20 minutes	6 to 24 hours	30 minutes	25 minutes	1 (2-inch) wedge

1¼ cups bread flour	3 TB. canola oil
¼ cup sugar	1 large egg
1¼ tsp. yeast	1 tsp. vanilla extract
½ tsp. salt	2 batches Double-Crumb Streusel
¼ cup whole milk	(recipe in Chapter 15)

1. In a large bowl, stir together flour, sugar, yeast, and salt. Stir in milk, canola oil, egg, and vanilla extract until completely combined.

2. Loosely cover with plastic wrap or a towel and let rise at room temperature for about 2 or 3 hours or until dough has doubled in size and surface is covered with large bubbles.

3. Refrigerate for at least 3 hours, or preferably overnight.

4. Preheat the oven to 375°F for 45 minutes. Line a 9-inch-round cake pan with a round piece of parchment paper and spray with nonstick cooking spray.

5. Press dough into the prepared pan, and sprinkle Double-Crumb Streusel evenly over top. Gently press streusel into dough. Let sit for 30 minutes.

6. Bake for about 20 to 25 minutes or until coffee cake is set and streusel is golden brown. Let cool in the pan for 45 minutes.

7. Run a knife along the inside edge to loosen coffee cake from the pan. Invert coffee cake onto a serving plate, cut into wedges, and serve.

Make it your own: Spread Cream Cheese Spread (recipe in Chapter 15) over dough before sprinkling with Double-Crumb Streusel.

BREAD HEAD

Did you know: vanilla is the second most expensive spice in the world, after saffron. The bean comes from an orchid that can only be pollinated one day a year.

Danish

Rich and buttery, and filled with jam or cheese, Danish pastries satisfy early morning hunger like nothing else. They're the quintessential sweet breakfast treat.

Yield:	Prep time:	Rest time:	Rise time:	Cook time:	Serving size:
12 Danish	15 minutes	6 to 24 hours	30 minutes	25 minutes	1 Danish

3 cups bread flour

$^1/_4$ cup sugar

1 TB. yeast

$1^1/_2$ tsp. salt

$^1/_2$ tsp. ground cardamom

$1^1/_4$ cup plus 1 TB. whole milk

2 large egg yolks

$^3/_4$ cup ($1^1/_2$ sticks) unsalted butter, softened

1 (8-oz.) pkg. cream cheese, softened

5 TB. sugar

1 TB. all-purpose flour

$^3/_4$ cup raspberry jam (optional)

1 batch Essential Egg Wash (recipe in Chapter 15)

$^1/_2$ cup apricot jam

2 TB. water

$^1/_2$ cup sliced almonds

1. In a large bowl, stir together bread flour, sugar, yeast, salt, and cardamom. Stir in milk and egg yolks until completely combined.

2. Loosely cover with plastic wrap or a towel and let rise at room temperature for about 2 or 3 hours or until dough has doubled in size and surface is covered with large bubbles.

3. Refrigerate for at least 3 hours, or preferably overnight.

4. In a small bowl, stir together softened butter and all-purpose flour until smooth. Spoon butter mixture on a piece of parchment paper or plastic wrap, and form into a 5×10-inch rectangle. Chill briefly until butter square is about the same texture as dough.

5. On a well-floured surface and with well-floured hands, roll dough into a 10×10-inch square. Place butter rectangle on one side of dough square, and fold over dough to seal into a package.

6. Rotate dough 90°, and roll into a 10×15-inch rectangle. Starting with the short end, fold dough into thirds by folding one end of dough into the center and then folding the other end over the first. This is the first turn.

7. Place dough on a plate, cover lightly with plastic wrap, and refrigerate for about 15 minutes.

8. Repeat 2 more turns, chilling dough briefly in between for about 15 minutes.

9. After completing the final turn, allow dough to rest for at least 1 hour in the refrigerator before continuing with recipe.

10. Preheat the oven to 375°F. Line 2 baking sheets with parchment paper.

11. On a well-floured work surface and with well-floured hands, divide dough in ¹/₂. Refrigerate ¹/₂ while you work with the other.

12. Roll out dough into an 8×12-inch rectangle. Cut dough in ¹/₂ horizontally and then make 3 vertical cuts to make 6 squares.

13. In a medium bowl, stir together cream cheese, sugar, and flour until smooth.

14. Spread 2 tablespoons cream cheese mixture onto each square. Spread raspberry jam (if using) over cream cheese.

15. Fold corners of each square to the center, and pinch to close into a diamond shape. Place Danish on the prepared baking sheet.

16. Brush Danish with Essential Egg Wash, and let rise for about 30 minutes. While Danish is rising, repeat with remaining piece of dough.

17. Bake Danish, one tray at a time, for about 15 minutes or until Danish are golden brown.

18. In a small saucepan over medium heat, heat apricot jam and water for about 2 minutes or until hot. Brush Danish with diluted jam, and sprinkle with sliced almonds.

19. Repeat with remaining Danish. Let cool and serve.

BAKER'S DOZEN

When chilling the dough in between turns, complete each step without too much time lapsing in between to ensure the best layering of dough and butter. Avoid chilling the dough for more than about 15 minutes to prevent the butter from getting cold and hard.

Croissants

Decadent and oh so buttery, these classic French pastries are well worth the extra effort.

Yield:	Prep time:	Rest time:	Rise time:	Cook time:	Serving size:
12 croissants	20 minutes	6 to 24 hours	30 minutes	25 minutes	1 croissant

3 cups bread flour

2 TB. sugar

1 TB. yeast

1½ tsp. salt

1 cup plus 1 TB. whole milk, lukewarm

½ cup lukewarm water

1½ cups (3 sticks) unsalted butter, softened

3 TB. all-purpose flour

1 batch Essential Egg Wash (recipe in Chapter 15)

1. In a large bowl, stir together bread flour, sugar, yeast, and salt. Stir in whole milk and water until completely combined.

2. Loosely cover with plastic wrap or a towel and let rise at room temperature for about 2 or 3 hours or until dough has doubled in size and surface is covered with large bubbles.

3. Refrigerate for at least 3 hours, or preferably overnight.

4. In a small bowl, stir together 1½ cups softened butter and all-purpose flour until smooth. Spoon butter mixture on a piece of parchment paper or plastic wrap, and form into a 5×10-inch rectangle. Chill briefly until butter square is about the same texture as dough.

5. On a well-floured surface and with well-floured hands, roll dough into a 10×10-inch square. Place butter rectangle on one side of dough square, and fold over dough to seal into a package.

6. Rotate dough 90°, and roll into a 10×15-inch rectangle. Starting with the short end, fold dough into thirds by folding one end of dough into the center and then folding the other end over the first. This is the first turn.

7. Place dough on a plate, cover lightly with plastic wrap, and refrigerate for about 15 minutes.

8. Repeat 2 more turns, chilling dough briefly in between for about 15 minutes.

9. After completing the final turn, allow dough to rest for at least 1 hour in refrigerator before continuing with recipe.

10. Place the oven racks in the upper-middle and lower-middle positions, and preheat the oven to 375°F. Line 2 baking sheets with parchment paper.

11. On a well-floured work surface and with well-floured hands, divide dough in $\frac{1}{2}$. Refrigerate $\frac{1}{2}$ while you work with the other.

12. Roll out dough into a 21×4-inch rectangle. Cut dough into 6 triangles with 6-inch bases.

13. Starting with the bottom of one triangle, roll up croissant and then curve ends in toward each other. Place on the prepared pan, and repeat with remaining triangles and then remaining dough.

14. Melt remaining $\frac{1}{4}$ cup butter and lightly brush over croissants. Lightly cover with plastic wrap and let rise for about 30 minutes or until dough feels jiggly.

15. Brush croissants with Essential Egg Wash, and bake for about 25 minutes or until golden brown. Serve warm.

BAKER'S DOZEN

To remind yourself of how many turns you've completed, use a baker's trick: after completing a turn, press your finger into the dough to mark each turn.

Holiday Breads

In This Chapter

- Holiday breads from around the world
- Dessert breads

The holidays are times to celebrate and share special treats with family and friends. And no holiday would be complete without many of the special breads that fill this chapter. They are beautiful, showpiece breads that will stand out on your table.

It's a shame that these delicious breads are often baked only once a year, but in the end, it only adds to their magic. Whether you bake one holiday bread a year or decide to indulge whenever the craving strikes, I hope you'll find a recipe (or two!) in this chapter that will become a favorite. And even if you think you're too busy to bake around the holidays, I promise these convenient no-knead recipes will easily fit in to your busy schedule. Your family and friends will be delighted and impressed by your effort. (But you don't have to tell them how easy it was!)

Holiday breads keep extraordinarily well, making them great make-ahead breads. Just be sure to keep them wrapped tightly if you're serving them within a few days. For longer storage, pop these breads in the freezer. Simply defrost in the refrigerator when ready to eat.

Simple Braiding

Many enriched breads, such as challah, display beautiful and elaborate braids. Here is an easy but striking looking braid. Try it with not only the Challah recipe in this chapter, but with the Easter Bread recipe as well.

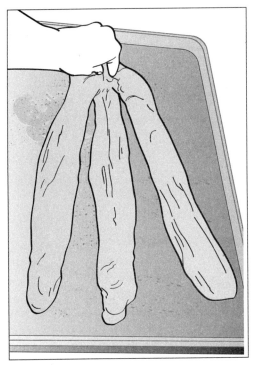

After rolling out three long pieces of dough, place them next to each other, slightly splayed, and pinch the pieces together on one end. Tuck the pinched end underneath.

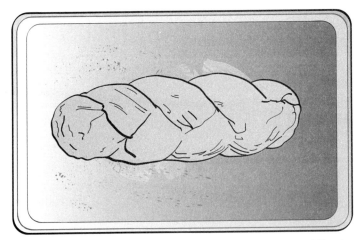

Pull the left piece over the middle piece, to become the new middle piece. Then, pull the right piece over the middle piece, which then becomes the new middle piece. Continue until you've worked your way to the end. Seal the end and tuck underneath.

Challah

With a deep golden and shiny crust, this challah's large braided shape makes it one of the most impressive breads. It's rich with egg and has a moist and tender crumb.

Yield:	Prep time:	Rest time:	Rise time:	Cook time:	Serving size:
1 challah	15 minutes	6 to 24 hours	20 minutes	35 minutes	1 (1-inch) piece

3½ cups all-purpose flour

⅓ cup sugar

2½ tsp. yeast

1½ tsp. salt

¾ cup lukewarm water

¼ cup vegetable oil

3 large eggs

1 large yolk

1 batch Essential Egg Wash (recipe in Chapter 15)

1. In a large bowl, stir together flour, sugar, yeast, and salt. Stir in water, vegetable oil, eggs, and egg yolk until completely combined.

2. Loosely cover with plastic wrap or a towel and let rise at room temperature for about 2 or 3 hours or until dough has doubled in size and surface is covered with large bubbles.

3. Refrigerate for at least 3 hours, or preferably overnight.

4. Preheat the oven to 400°F. Line a baking sheet with parchment paper and sprinkle with flour.

5. On a well-floured work surface and with well-floured hands, shape dough into a smooth ball. Divide ball into 3 pieces.

6. Roll each piece into a 16-inch rope and place lengthwise on the prepared baking sheet. Pinch pieces together on one end, and tuck under slightly.

7. Braid ropes together, pinching the ends together and tucking under.

8. Brush challah with Essential Egg Wash and let rest for 20 minutes. Brush loaf with Essential Egg Wash a second time and bake for about 35 minutes or until challah is a deep golden brown and an instant-read thermometer inserted into center of loaf registers about 195°F to 200°F.

9. Let cool on the baking sheet for 15 minutes and then transfer loaf to a cooling rack to cool completely. Cut into slices, and serve.

Make it your own: For a raisin-infused challah, soak $1/2$ cup raisins in 1 cup hot water for 1 hour. Drain raisins and add to dough in step 1.

BREAD HEAD

Challah is a special braided bread eaten by Jews on the Sabbath and holidays.

Easter Bread

This bread is the easiest of the sweetened yeast breads to make and has a very deep golden crust. It's lightly sweetened and makes excellent thick sliced toast.

Yield:	Prep time:	Rest time:	Rise time:	Cook time:	Serving size:
1 (9-inch-round) loaf	10 minutes	6 to 24 hours	30 minutes	30 minutes	1 (1-inch) slice

2¹/₂ cups all-purpose flour

¹/₃ cup sugar

1¹/₂ tsp. yeast

¹/₄ tsp. salt

1 cup whole milk

6 TB. unsalted butter, melted

1 large egg

1 batch Essential Egg Wash (recipe in Chapter 15)

1. In a large bowl, stir together flour, sugar, yeast, and salt. Stir in milk, melted butter, and egg until completely combined.

2. Loosely cover with plastic wrap or a towel and let rise at room temperature for about 2 or 3 hours or until dough has doubled in size and surface is covered with large bubbles.

3. Refrigerate for at least 3 hours, or preferably overnight.

4. Preheat the oven to 350°F for 45 minutes. Spray a 9-inch cake pan with nonstick cooking spray.

5. On a well-floured surface and with well-floured hands, shape dough into a 8-inch disc and place in the pan. Brush top with Essential Egg Wash and let sit for about 30 minutes.

6. Brush top with Essential Egg Wash a second time, and bake for about 30 minutes or until bread is set, top is a deep golden brown, and an instant-read thermometer inserted into center of loaf registers about 195°F.

7. Let bread cool in the pan for 15 minutes and then transfer loaf to a cooling rack to cool completely. Cut into slices, and serve.

Make it your own: For a traditional and flavorful twist, mix 2 teaspoons aniseed and $1/2$ teaspoon anise extract into the dough in step 1. For a colorful and decorative touch, gently press 1 Easter egg into the top of the dough (in the center), just before baking.

BREAD HEAD

This addicting buttery bread is also known as Italian, Greek, or Russian Easter bread. The traditional Easter egg that's placed in this holiday bread symbolizes rebirth and also celebrates the end of the prohibitions of Lent.

Hot Cross Buns

These soft, sweetened rolls are traditionally served at Easter. They are dotted with currants and candied citron, and a vanilla glaze gives the bread its hallmark "cross" design.

Yield:	Prep time:	Rest time:	Rise time:	Cook time:	Serving size:
7 buns	45 minutes	6 to 24 hours	45 minutes	30 minutes	1 bun

$1/2$ cup currants

2 TB. water

$2^1/2$ cups all-purpose flour

$1/2$ cup sugar

3 TB. *candied citron*

2 tsp. yeast

$1^1/2$ tsp. salt

$1/4$ tsp. cinnamon

$1/4$ tsp. nutmeg

$1/2$ cup whole milk

6 TB. unsalted butter, melted

2 eggs

1 batch Essential Egg Wash (recipe in Chapter 15)

1 batch Vanilla Glaze (recipe in Chapter 15)

1. In a small saucepan over medium heat, combine currants and water. Cook for about 1 minute or until currants are just warmed through. Set aside for about 30 minutes to cool and allow currants to absorb water.

2. In a large bowl, stir together flour, sugar, candied citron, yeast, salt, cinnamon, and nutmeg. Stir in milk, melted butter, and eggs until completely combined.

3. Loosely cover with plastic wrap or a towel and let rise at room temperature for about 2 or 3 hours or until dough has doubled in size and surface is covered with large bubbles.

4. Refrigerate for at least 3 hours, or preferably overnight.

5. Preheat the oven to 350°F. Coat a 9-inch cake pan with nonstick cooking spray.

6. On a lightly floured surface and with lightly floured hands, divide dough into 7 equal portions. Roll each piece into a ball and place in the pan.

7. Brush with Essential Egg Wash and let rise for 45 minutes.

8. Brush with Essential Egg Wash a second time, and bake for about 30 minutes or until buns are golden brown and an instant-read thermometer inserted into center bun reads about 185°F.

9. Let buns cool 30 minutes in the pan and then drizzle a Vanilla Glaze "cross" over each bun. Serve.

LOAF LINGO

Candied citron is made from the lemonlike fruit of the citron shrub, an evergreen native to India. The thick, yellow rind is candied by cooking it in a sugar syrup.

Stollen

This slightly sweet breadlike cake is filled with a bounty of dried and candied fruits and nuts. A heavy dusting of confectioners' sugar makes it festive.

Yield:	Prep time:	Rest time:	Rise time:	Cook time:	Serving size:
1 (12-inch) stollen	45 minutes	6 to 24 hours	30 minutes	35 minutes	1 (2-inch) slice

³/₄ cup currants	2 TB. dried apricots, diced
2 TB. orange juice	2 TB. dried prunes, diced
3 TB. dark rum	4 TB. candied citron
2³/₄ cups all-purpose flour	³/₄ cup sliced almonds
¹/₃ cup sugar	³/₄ cup lukewarm milk
1³/₄ tsp. yeast	7 TB. unsalted butter, melted
³/₄ tsp. salt	2 eggs
¹/₂ tsp. nutmeg	1 tsp. vanilla extract
³/₄ cup golden raisins	1 cup confectioners' sugar

1. In a small saucepan over medium heat, cook currants, orange juice, and rum for about 2 minutes or until heated through. Set aside for 30 minutes to cool and allow currants to absorb liquid.

2. In a large bowl, stir together flour, sugar, yeast, salt, nutmeg, raisins, apricots, prunes, candied citron, and almonds. Stir in milk, melted butter, eggs, and vanilla extract until completely combined.

3. Loosely cover with plastic wrap and let rise at room temperature for about 2 or 3 hours or until dough has doubled in size and surface is covered with large bubbles.

4. Refrigerate for at least 3 hours, or preferably overnight.

5. Preheat the oven to 350°F. Line a baking sheet with parchment paper.

6. On a lightly floured surface roll out dough to a 12×10-inch rectangle. Brush with 1 tablespoon melted butter.

7. With lightly floured hands, start with the long end of dough and fold dough to the middle. Fold over the other end, overlapping the dough by about 1 inch.

8. Transfer stollen to the prepared baking sheet. Brush with remaining 1 tablespoon melted butter and let rise 30 minutes.

9. Bake for about 35 minutes or until stollen is deep golden brown and an instant-read thermometer inserted into center reads about 185°F.

10. Transfer stollen to a cooling rack. While still warm, sift confectioners' sugar over top. Let cool completely, cut into slices, and serve.

BREAD HEAD

Stollen is a traditional German fruitcake usually eaten at Christmastime. It's been recorded in history as far back as the 1400s.

Panettone

This enriched bread is often served at Christmas. It's traditionally a tall bread, studded with raisins and candied citron. Sweet marsala wine flavors the dough.

Yield:	Prep time:	Rest time:	Rise time:	Cook time:	Serving size:
2 panettone	45 minutes	6 to 24 hours	45 minutes	45 minutes	1 (1-inch) wedge

3¼ cups all-purpose flour

1 cup candied citron

1 cup raisins

⅔ cup plus 1 TB. sugar

½ cup golden raisins

1 TB. plus 1 tsp. yeast

1 TB. lemon zest

¾ tsp. salt

¾ cup sweet marsala wine

½ cup whole milk, lukewarm

½ cup (1 stick) unsalted butter, melted

3 large eggs

2 large egg yolks

1 TB. lemon juice

1 batch Essential Egg Wash (recipe in Chapter 15)

1. In a large bowl, stir together flour, candied citron, raisins, sugar, golden raisins, yeast, lemon zest, and salt. Stir in marsala wine, milk, melted butter, eggs, egg yolks, and lemon juice until completely combined.

2. Refrigerate dough for at least 3 hours, or preferably overnight.

3. Preheat the oven to 375°F. Spray the bottoms of 2 (15-ounce) coffee cans with nonstick cooking spray. Line the inside of each can with parchment paper, leaving a 1-inch collar above the rim of the can. Line a baking sheet with parchment paper.

4. Divide dough in ½ and drop into the bottom of each prepared can. Place on the parchment paper–lined baking sheet.

5. Brush top of panettones with Essential Egg Wash, and let rise at room temperature for 45 minutes. Bake for about 45 minutes or until top is deep golden brown and an instant-read thermometer inserted into center registers 190°F.

6. Let panettone cool in the can. When ready to serve, remove from the can, slice into wedges, and serve.

BAKER'S DOZEN

Because of its beautiful tall shape, panettone makes a wonderful gift. If that's your plan, try using a special panettone paper mold. These are made to use in lieu of the coffee can and come in pretty, festive designs.

Baba au Rhum

This dessert is a perfect choice when you want a spectacular presentation. The ring-shape rum-soaked cake is filled with sweetened whipped cream and fresh berries. It's over the top!

Yield:	Prep time:	Rest time:	Rise time:	Cook time:	Serving size:
1 (9-inch) baba	20 minutes	6 to 24 hours	60 minutes	25 to 30 minutes	1 (2-inch) wedge

2¼ cups bread flour

5 tsp. yeast

2 TB. sugar

½ tsp. salt

½ cup (1 stick) plus 1 TB. unsalted butter, melted

¼ cup whole milk, lukewarm

3 large eggs

1 large egg yolk

1 TB. orange zest

1 batch Rum Soaking Syrup (recipe in Chapter 15)

1 batch Sweet Whipped Cream (recipe in Chapter 15)

2 cups mixed berries (blueberries, raspberries, strawberries)

1. In a large bowl, stir together flour, yeast, sugar, and salt. Stir in melted butter, milk, eggs, egg yolk, and orange zest until completely combined.

2. Loosely cover with plastic wrap or a towel and let rise at room temperature for about 2 or 3 hours or until dough has doubled in size and surface is covered with large bubbles.

3. Refrigerate for at least 3 hours, or preferably overnight.

4. Preheat the oven to 375°F. Coat a 9-inch Bundt pan with nonstick cooking spray.

5. With lightly floured hands, shape dough into a cylinder and place dough in the prepared pan. Lightly brush top with water and let dough sit for about 1 hour to rise slightly.

6. Bake for 25 to 30 minutes or until top is golden and baba is set. Let cool in the pan for 30 minutes and then invert onto a cooling rack.

7. Gently place baba back into the pan, and pour 1¼ cups warm Rum Soaking Syrup over baba. Let syrup soak into baba for 2 hours.

8. Invert baba onto a serving platter, and brush with remaining Rum Soaking Syrup. Fill the center of ring with Sweet Whipped Cream and berries. Serve.

BREAD HEAD

In French, *baba* means "falling over" or "dizzy." No wonder, given the amount of liquor it's soaked with!

Quick Breads

Need to get a bread on the table but don't have time to wait for the dough to rise? Welcome to the magic of quick breads! Of all the no-knead breads, quick breads are undoubtedly the fastest. Just mix and bake. Pumpkin bread, cornbread, and soda bread all fall in this category of super-easy breads. And as promised, no mixers are required to make these recipes.

Quick breads don't need to rise before you bake them. Instead of yeast, these breads use chemical leaveners such as baking powder and baking soda. As soon as the batter or dough hits the heat of the oven, the leaveners immediately go to work to make the bread rise. And because these breads don't develop much gluten, the result is a very tender bread. Also, many quick bread mixtures are sweeter and more like a batter than a dough. In all these ways, quick breads are in a class all their own.

These quick bread recipes in Part 4 fully round out your bread-making repertoire. With recipes that can be mixed and ready to bake in a matter of minutes, it doesn't get any "quicker" than this!

Quick Loaf Breads

In This Chapter

- The rise of quick breads
- Quick bread rules
- Quick loaf bread favorites

Nothing says "thank you" or "welcome" like the gift of a freshly baked loaf of zucchini or cranberry-walnut bread. And as they bake, you're rewarded with the scents of warm spices, fruit, and chocolate that blanket you in cozy comfort. The breads in this chapter are also family favorites and make the perfect choice for a picnic, bake sale, teatime, or gift.

Thanks to the super-fast, quick bread method—no need to wait for the dough to rise!—you can get these tasty breads in the oven in no time flat.

On the Fast Track

We weren't always privileged enough to enjoy the ease of a quick bread. In the history of bread-making, quick breads are a relatively new development. For years, yeast was the primary substance used in bread-making to make doughs rise. But as we know, yeast needs time to grow.

Over time, both serendipity in the kitchen and our "need for speed" fueled the search for an instant leavener that would create the same gaseous bubbles as yeast. Early bakers experimented with leaveners such as pearlash, saleratus, and hartshorn, but all these left unpleasant flavors in the baked bread.

BREAD HEAD

The primitive leavener hartshorn was originally made from the ground antlers of a male deer, or hart. As it baked, the gases produced by hartshorn gave off the odor of ammonia. That's a far cry from the sweet cinnamon and spice emanating from today's ovens!

During the nineteenth century, the modern chemical leaveners we know today, baking soda and baking powder, became available, and a whole new world of "quick" baking was at our fingertips.

Mixing

For the loaf pan quick breads in this chapter, we use one of the easiest and most common methods for the quick bread mixing, simply mixing the dry ingredients into the wet ingredients. First you whisk together the eggs and sugar to combine and incorporate air to help lighten the bread. Then you add a liquid fat and the rest of the liquid ingredients. Finally, you fold the dry ingredients into the wet ingredients until just moistened.

When you add the dry ingredients, mix until no dry pockets of flour remain, but stop before it's completely smooth. Unless otherwise stated, it's very important not to overmix the batter because a typical yeast bread benefits from gluten formation, which helps it rise properly and create that wonderful chewy texture. Quick breads, on the other hand, don't need to develop extra gluten because they usually contain eggs for structure.

The texture of a quick bread should also be more tender and cakelike than a yeast bread. Overmixing a quick bread batter pushes around the flour proteins, which develop gluten and make the quick bread tough. Here, less is more!

It's also important to remember that unlike the make-ahead bread doughs in the preceding chapters, quick bread batters and doughs are meant to be baked immediately after mixing. Chemical leaveners start to react as soon as they're moistened and will begin to lose their effectiveness after a while. It's not a good idea to leave the batters on the counter or store them in the fridge.

Dry mixes, on the other hand, can be made ahead to save time. Combine the flour, leaveners, salt, and spices, and store in an airtight container in a cool, dry place until ready to use. These make-ahead dry mixes also make thoughtful gifts. Tuck a copy of the recipe into the container, tie with a pretty bow, and you're all set!

Knowing When It's Done

A baking quick bread is more fragile than a typical yeast bread. Before it completely sets, it's vulnerable to being bumped or to extreme changes in the oven temperature. It's a good idea not to move it around after it goes into the oven, or to open and close the oven door too much. Doing so may cause the bread to sink!

When a quick bread loaf is done, the top of the loaf feels just firm to the touch. To ensure the loaf is cooked through, insert a toothpick or cake tester into the center of the loaf. If it comes out clean, the bread is done. Having a few crumbs is also okay.

DOUGH DON'T

Be careful when checking the loaf. If you press the top down too hard before it sets, the top may sink slightly.

As the quick bread loaf bakes and rises, sometimes it develops a signature "pound cake" split down the middle of the loaf. This split often stays moist until the very last few minutes of baking and is the last part to finish baking.

Cool It

A few of the quick bread loaves are yummy when eaten fresh from the oven, but many are best when allowed to cool completely. For these breads, a sufficient cooling time allows subtle flavors to develop. The texture also improves after all the hot steam has had a chance to escape. For breads that are to be iced, it's imperative that the bread be completely cool before icing.

Loaf quick breads have remarkable keeping qualities if they're stored properly. Keep leftovers under a cake dome or place on a plate and wrap in plastic wrap. As with any food, however, take special care during hot summer months or in humid climates. Storing a wrapped loaf in the refrigerator may be the better option in such cases.

Quick breads also freeze very well, which makes them great make-ahead breads. Simply wrap in plastic wrap, place in a freezer bag, and pop it in the freezer. Just defrost when ready to eat!

Lemon Zinger Poppy Bread

This fragrant loaf gets a generous drizzle of tart Lemon Pucker Icing. Poppy seeds add a nutty crunch.

Yield:	Prep time:	Cook time:	Serving size:
1 (8$1/2$×4$1/2$×3-inch) loaf	20 minutes	55 minutes	1 ($3/4$-inch) slice

1$3/4$ cups all-purpose flour

2 TB. poppy seeds

1$1/2$ tsp. baking powder

$1/4$ tsp. baking soda

$1/4$ tsp. salt

1 cup sugar

2 large eggs

2 TB. lemon *zest*

$1/2$ cup (1 stick) unsalted butter, melted

$2/3$ cup sour cream

1 batch Lemon Pucker Icing (recipe in Chapter 15)

1. Preheat the oven to 350°F. Coat a 8$1/2$×4$1/2$×3-inch loaf pan with nonstick cooking spray.

2. In a medium bowl, whisk together flour, poppy seeds, baking powder, baking soda, and salt. Set aside.

3. In a large bowl, whisk together sugar, eggs, and lemon zest for about 30 seconds or until lightened. Whisk in melted butter and sour cream. Fold in flour mixture until just moistened.

4. Spoon batter into the prepared pan, and bake for about 55 minutes or until golden, firm, and a toothpick inserted into middle of loaf comes out clean.

5. Cool loaf in the pan for 20 minutes. Remove from the pan and cool completely on a wire rack.

6. Spread Lemon Pucker Icing over top of cooled bread, allowing it to drip down sides. Allow icing to set before serving.

LOAF LINGO

Zest is the outer peel of a citrus fruit. It's packed with flavor and aromatic oils. The best tool to use to get the most zest is a zester, a Microplane, or the fine holes of a box grater. Gently scrape the colorful outer skin away, being sure to avoid the white pith underneath, which tends to be bitter.

Banana-Rama Bread

Who can resist the irresistible combination of sweet banana, cinnamon, and crunchy walnuts?

Yield:	Prep time:	Cook time:	Serving size:
1 (8¹/₂×4¹/₂×3-inch) loaf	20 minutes	75 minutes	1 (³/₄-inch) slice

1³/₄ cups all-purpose flour	6 TB. unsalted butter, melted
2 tsp. baking powder	¹/₄ cup sour cream
¹/₂ tsp. ground cinnamon	1 tsp. vanilla extract
¹/₂ tsp. salt	2 medium bananas, peeled and mashed
¹/₄ tsp. baking soda	³/₄ cup chopped walnuts
³/₄ cup sugar	
2 large eggs	

1. Preheat the oven to 350°F. Coat a 8¹/₂×4¹/₂×3-inch loaf pan with nonstick cooking spray.

2. In a medium bowl, whisk together flour, baking powder, cinnamon, salt, and baking soda. Set aside.

3. In a large bowl, whisk together sugar and eggs for about 30 seconds or until lightened. Whisk in butter, sour cream, and vanilla extract. Stir in mashed bananas. Fold in flour mixture and ¹/₂ cup walnuts until just moistened.

4. Pour batter into the prepared pan, and sprinkle remaining ¹/₄ cup walnuts on top. Bake for about 70 to 75 minutes or until golden, firm, and a toothpick inserted into middle of loaf comes out clean.

5. Cool loaf in the pan for 45 minutes. Remove from the pan and cool completely or cut into slices and serve warm.

BAKER'S DOZEN

To reap the most banana flavor, be sure your bananas are super-ripe. The perfect ripe banana should be yellow with brown spots. If you have too many ripe bananas to use right away, good news: they freeze very well. Simply toss the unpeeled bananas in a freezer bag and then into the freezer.

Moist Zucchini Bread

Spicy cinnamon and pungent cloves infuse lots of flavor into this loaf, which owes its moistness to both the vegetable oil and fresh zucchini.

Yield:	Prep time:	Cook time:	Serving size:
1 (8¹/₂×4¹/₂×3-inch) loaf	20 minutes	60 minutes	1 (³/₄-inch) slice

1¹/₂ cups all-purpose flour

2¹/₂ tsp. baking powder

1³/₄ tsp. ground cinnamon

1 tsp. ground cloves

¹/₂ tsp. salt

1 cup sugar

2 large eggs

¹/₂ cup vegetable oil

1 tsp. vanilla extract

2 medium zucchini, peeled and finely shredded (about 2 cups)

³/₄ cup chopped walnuts

1. Preheat the oven to 350°F. Coat a 8¹/₂×4¹/₂×3-inch loaf pan with nonstick cooking spray.

2. In a medium bowl, whisk together flour, baking powder, cinnamon, cloves, and salt. Set aside.

3. In a large bowl, whisk together sugar and eggs for about 30 seconds or until lightened. Whisk in vegetable oil and vanilla extract. Stir in zucchini until combined. Fold in flour mixture and walnuts until just moistened.

4. Pour batter into the prepared pan, and bake for 55 to 60 minutes or until golden, firm, and a toothpick inserted into middle of loaf comes out clean.

5. Cool loaf in the pan for 45 minutes. Remove from the pan and cool completely on a wire rack before serving.

Make it your own: Spread slices of this bread with your favorite flavor of Cream Cheese Spread (recipe in Chapter 15).

DOUGH DON'T

Try to avoid large zucchini, which tend to contain large, chewy, and fibrous seeds. If your zucchini does have seeds, simply scrape them out with a spoon.

Pumpkin Spice Bread

Sit back with a mulled cider and let the cozy aromas of fall waft through your home as this loaf bakes. Every bite of this headily spiced family-favorite bread is pure comfort.

Yield:	Prep time:	Cook time:	Serving size:
1 (8¹/₂×4¹/₂×3-inch) loaf	20 minutes	60 minutes	1 (³/₄-inch) slice

1³/₄ cups all-purpose flour

1¹/₂ tsp. ground cinnamon

1¹/₂ tsp. ground nutmeg

1 tsp. ground cloves

1 tsp. baking powder

¹/₂ tsp. baking soda

¹/₂ tsp. salt

1¹/₄ cups sugar

2 large eggs

¹/₂ cup (1 stick) unsalted butter, melted

1¹/₄ cups solid-pack canned pumpkin

1. Preheat the oven to 350°F. Coat a 8¹/₂×4¹/₂×3-inch loaf pan with nonstick cooking spray.

2. In a medium bowl, whisk together flour, cinnamon, nutmeg, cloves, baking powder, baking soda, and salt. Set aside.

3. In a large bowl, whisk together sugar and eggs for about 30 seconds or until lightened. Whisk in melted butter and pumpkin. Fold in flour mixture until just moistened.

4. Pour batter into the prepared pan, and bake for about 60 minutes or until golden, firm, and a toothpick inserted into middle of loaf comes out clean.

5. Cool loaf in the pan for 45 minutes. Remove from the pan and cool completely on a wire rack, or cut into slices and serve warm.

Make it your own: Serve cooled pumpkin bread slices with your favorite flavor of Cream Cheese Spread (recipe in Chapter 15).

BAKER'S DOZEN

Be sure to use pure pumpkin purée for this recipe, not pumpkin pie filling, which has added spices and flavorings that won't work well with this bread.

Orange Cranberry Walnut Bread

Bursts of tart, juicy cranberries brighten up this classic quick bread. The orange zest adds a flavorful citrus note.

Yield:	Prep time:	Cook time:	Serving size:
1 (8½×4½×3-inch) loaf	20 minutes	70 minutes	1 (¾-inch) slice

2 cups all-purpose flour	6 TB. unsalted butter, melted
2 tsp. baking powder	½ cup sour cream
½ tsp. salt	1 tsp. vanilla extract
1 cup sugar	1½ cups fresh or frozen unthawed
2 large eggs	whole cranberries
1 TB. orange zest	⅓ cup chopped walnuts

1. Preheat the oven to 350°F. Coat a 8½×4½×3-inch loaf pan with nonstick cooking spray.

2. In a medium bowl, whisk together flour, baking powder, and salt. Set aside.

3. In a large bowl, whisk together sugar, eggs, and orange zest for about 30 seconds or until lightened. Whisk in melted butter, sour cream, and vanilla extract. Fold in flour mixture, cranberries, and walnuts until just moistened.

4. Pour batter into the prepared pan, and bake for 65 to 70 minutes or until golden, firm, and a toothpick inserted into middle of loaf comes out clean.

5. Cool loaf in the pan for 45 minutes. Remove from the pan and cool completely on a wire rack or cut into slices and serve warm.

BREAD HEAD

Cranberries are packed with vitamin C. During the fall cranberry season, pop extra bags of fresh cranberries in the freezer so you can enjoy this bread year round!

Spicy Gingerbread

Bring the holidays home anytime of the year with the combination of ginger, cinnamon, and cloves. Chock-full of molasses, this incredibly moist bread is deeply flavorful and immensely satisfying.

Yield:	Prep time:	Cook time:	Serving size:
1 (8×8-inch) pan	25 minutes	45 minutes	1 (2$^1/_2$-inch) square

2$^1/_4$ cups all-purpose flour

2 tsp. ground ginger

1$^1/_2$ tsp. baking soda

1 tsp. ground cinnamon

$^1/_2$ tsp. salt

$^1/_4$ tsp. ground cloves

$^3/_4$ cup firmly packed light brown sugar

2 large eggs

$^1/_2$ cup (1 stick) unsalted butter, melted

$^3/_4$ cup molasses

$^3/_4$ cup hot water

1 batch Sweet Whipped Cream (recipe in Chapter 15; optional)

1. Preheat the oven to 350°F. Coat a 8×8-inch baking pan with nonstick cooking spray.

2. In a medium bowl, whisk together flour, ginger, baking soda, cinnamon, salt, and cloves. Set aside.

3. In a large bowl, whisk together brown sugar and eggs until lightened, about 30 seconds. Whisk in melted butter, molasses, and hot water. Whisk in flour mixture until smooth.

4. Pour batter into the prepared pan, and bake for 40 to 45 minutes or until golden, firm, and a toothpick inserted into middle of loaf comes out clean.

5. Cool loaf in the pan for 20 minutes. Remove from the pan, cut into squares, and serve warm with Sweet Whipped Cream (if using) or cool completely in the pan.

DOUGH DON'T

While most of the batters in this book are just stirred together at the end to keep the crumb tender, this recipe is an exception. The wetter-than-usual batter needs to be whisked to smooth out all the lumps. Also, while this liquid-y batter bakes, it's particularly fragile until the crumb sets. To avoid a sunken center, be gentle when opening and closing the oven door, and try to avoid checking for doneness until close to the end.

Double Chocolate Loaf Bread

Packed with chocolate chips, this decadent loaf is pure chocolate overload. It'll satisfy even the die-hard chocoholic.

Yield:	Prep time:	Cook time:	Serving size:
1 (8½×4½×3-inch) loaf	20 minutes	70 minutes	1 (¾-inch) slice

1½ cups all-purpose flour	2 large eggs
½ cup unsweetened cocoa powder	⅔ cup vegetable oil
1¼ tsp. baking soda	1 cup sour cream
½ tsp. salt	1½ tsp. vanilla extract
1¼ cups sugar	¾ cup bittersweet chocolate chips

1. Preheat the oven to 350°F. Coat a 8½×4½×3-inch loaf pan with nonstick cooking spray.

2. Sift flour, cocoa powder, baking soda, and salt into a medium bowl. Set aside.

3. In a large bowl, whisk together sugar and eggs for about 30 seconds or until lightened. Whisk in vegetable oil, sour cream, and vanilla extract. Fold in flour mixture and chocolate chips until just moistened.

4. Pour batter into the prepared pan, and bake for about 60 to 70 minutes or until firm and a toothpick inserted into middle of loaf comes out clean.

5. Cool loaf in the pan completely.

Make it your own: Mix up the chips! Semisweet, milk chocolate, white chocolate, peanut butter, or even butterscotch chips all work well here.

BREAD HEAD

When the original chocolate chip cookie recipe (Toll House) was developed, chocolate chunks were used because chocolate chips hadn't been invented yet! In 1939, the Nestlés company created and marketed the chocolate morsel, or chocolate chip, and the rest is history.

Coconut Lime Tea Bread

Light and tropical in flavor, this bread is the perfect accompaniment to a cup of tea. The lime zest makes it uniquely refreshing.

Yield:	Prep time:	Cook time:	Serving size:
1 (8¹/₂×4¹/₂×3-inch) loaf	20 minutes	60 minutes	1 (³/₄-inch) slice

1¹/₂ cups all-purpose flour

³/₄ cup sweetened shredded coconut

1¹/₂ tsp. baking powder

¹/₄ tsp. baking soda

¹/₄ tsp. salt

1 cup sugar

2 large eggs

2 TB. lime zest

¹/₂ cup (1 stick) unsalted butter, melted

²/₃ cup sour cream

1. Preheat the oven to 350°F. Coat a 8¹/₂×4¹/₂×3-inch loaf pan with nonstick spray.

2. In a medium bowl, whisk together flour, coconut, baking powder, baking soda, and salt. Set aside.

3. In a large bowl, whisk together sugar, eggs, and lime zest for about 30 seconds or until lightened. Whisk in melted butter and sour cream. Fold in flour mixture until just moistened.

4. Pour batter into the prepared pan, and bake for about 55 to 60 minutes or until golden, firm, and a toothpick inserted into middle of loaf comes out clean.

5. Cool loaf in the pan for 45 minutes. Remove from the pan and cool completely on a wire rack.

BREAD HEAD

The word *coconut* originates from the Spanish and Portuguese word *coco*, which means "monkey face." These explorers thought the fruit resembled a monkey's face with its brown hairy covering and round indentations that resembled eyes.

Buttermilk Corn Bread

Slightly sweet corn flavor and tangy buttermilk make this bread the perfect complement to spicy dishes such as chili.

Yield:	Prep time:	Cook time:	Serving size:
1 (8×8-inch) pan	15 minutes	40 minutes	1 (2½-inch) square

1½ cups all-purpose flour

1¼ cups yellow cornmeal

2½ tsp. baking powder

¾ tsp. salt

½ tsp. baking soda

¾ cup sugar

3 large eggs

¾ cup (1½ sticks) unsalted butter, melted

1 cup buttermilk

1. Preheat the oven to 375°F. Coat an 8×8-inch baking pan with nonstick cooking spray.

2. In a medium bowl, whisk together flour, cornmeal, baking powder, salt, and baking soda. Set aside.

3. In a large bowl, whisk together sugar and eggs for about 30 seconds or until lightened. Whisk in melted butter and buttermilk. Fold in flour mixture until just moistened.

4. Pour batter into the prepared pan, and bake for 35 to 40 minutes or until golden, firm, and a toothpick inserted into middle of bread comes out clean.

5. Cool loaf in the pan for 10 minutes before serving.

Make it your own: Add a gourmet touch to this bread by serving it with Honey-Butter Spread (recipe in Chapter 15).

BAKER'S DOZEN

If you need to feed a crowd, this bread can easily be doubled. Reduce the oven temperature to 350°F, use a 9×13-inch pan, and increase the baking time to about 45 to 55 minutes.

Irish Tea Bread

Whiskey-soaked raisins and black tea pack a flavorful punch in this moist, rich bread. Toast and butter any leftovers for a tasty breakfast treat.

Yield:	Prep time:	Cook time:	Serving size:
1 (8¹/₂×4¹/₂×3-inch) loaf	80 minutes	60 minutes	1 (³/₄-inch) slice

2 cups golden raisins	³/₄ cup plus 2 TB. firmly packed light brown sugar
¹/₂ cup whiskey	2 large eggs
¹/₂ cup brewed black tea	1 tsp. lemon zest
2 cups all-purpose flour	1 tsp. orange zest
1¹/₂ tsp. baking powder	2 TB. unsalted butter, melted
³/₄ tsp. salt	

1. In a small saucepan over medium heat, bring raisins, whiskey, and tea to just simmering. Remove from heat and let raisins soak, uncovered, for 1 hour.

2. Preheat the oven to 350°F. Coat a 8¹/₂×4¹/₂×3-inch loaf pan with nonstick cooking spray.

3. In a medium bowl, whisk together flour, baking powder, and salt. Set aside.

4. In a large bowl, whisk together brown sugar, eggs, lemon zest, and orange zest for about 30 seconds or until lightened. Whisk in melted butter, and stir in raisin mixture. Stir in flour mixture until just moistened.

5. Pour batter into the prepared pan, and bake for 55 to 60 minutes or until deep golden brown, firm, and a toothpick inserted into middle of loaf comes out clean.

6. Cool loaf in the pan for 30 minutes. Remove from the pan and serve slightly warm or completely cool on a wire rack.

Make it your own: You can replace the raisins with any combination of chopped dried fruits. This bread is also delicious with vanilla or lemony Cream Cheese Spread (recipe in Chapter 15).

BREAD HEAD

This traditional Irish tea bread is also known as *Barm Brack*. Years ago in Ireland on Halloween, this bread was used to give people's fortunes. Small tokens, each symbolizing a particular fortune, were baked into the bread. Depending on which token people found in their slices, they would then receive that fortune. For example, a coin signified good luck, while a piece of cloth meant very bad luck.

Cheddar-Chive Beer Bread

Beer, cheddar, and chives form a flavorful trio in this cinch-to-make bread. As the bread cools, the yeasty flavor from the beer mellows.

Yield:	Prep time:	Cook time:	Serving size:
1 (8¹/₂×4¹/₂×3-inch) loaf	15 minutes	45 minutes	1 (³/₄-inch) slice

3 cups all-purpose flour	¹/₄ cup chopped fresh chives
1 TB. baking powder	1 (12-oz.) can beer (1¹/₂ cups)
4 tsp. sugar	2 TB. unsalted butter, melted
1 tsp. salt	
1¹/₄ cups mild cheddar cheese, shredded	

1. Preheat the oven to 375°F. Coat a 8¹/₂×4¹/₂×3-inch loaf pan with nonstick cooking spray.

2. In a large bowl, whisk together flour, baking powder, sugar, and salt.

3. Stir in cheddar cheese, chives, beer, and melted butter until batter is moistened.

4. Pour into the prepared pan, and bake for about 45 minutes or until golden and firm, and a toothpick inserted into middle of bread comes out clean.

5. Cool loaf in the pan for 10 minutes. Remove from the pan and serve slightly warm or cool completely.

DOUGH DON'T

Don't spend a fortune on the beer you use here. Any no-frills beer will do, as long as it's mildly flavored. A dark beer will taste too robust and overwhelm the bread.

Shaped Quick Breads

In This Chapter

- Homemade soda breads
- Serving up scones
- Baking biscuits

A free-form quick bread is simply a quick bread whose dough is sturdy enough to be shaped by hand and doesn't need the support of a pan to bake. These wonderfully simple breads are the easiest and quickest to mix together and to get in (and out) of the oven at a moment's notice.

From hearty Irish soda breads or biscuits you can serve meal-side, to breakfast favorites such as scones, free-form quick breads fit every occasion.

Irish Soda Bread

Around St. Patrick's Day, you can't miss the plethora of Irish soda breads in bakery windows. While the Irish may not have invented this particular bread, Irish soda bread has been an important element of Irish cuisine since the nineteenth century when baking soda became the leavener of choice. Yeast breads never took hold in Ireland like soda breads. This was most likely due to Ireland's cool, damp climate, which isn't suitable for yeast to rise or for growing high-protein (gluten-forming) wheat. Breads made with baking soda were quick and reliable and remain popular choices today.

It's customary to make two signature slashes in the shape of a cross on the top of the soda bread before baking. This helps the dense bread expand properly in the oven.

Shaping and Baking

Free-form quick breads aren't as wet as no-knead yeast doughs; however, they can still be pretty sticky. Shaping the loaf on a well-floured surface and using well-floured hands helps the dough from sticking to your hands.

Try not to work the dough too much or it will toughen the final texture.

BAKER'S DOZEN

You don't have to take a quick bread's temperature to know it's done. Seeing that the bread is golden and firm to the touch is usually enough, and a skewer inserted into the center should come out with just a few moist crumbs. As with all breads, allowing the loaf to cool on a cooling rack keeps the bottom crust crisp.

Irish Soda Bread

Flavored with sweet currants and aromatic caraway seeds, this peasant bread can be served any day of the year.

Yield:	Prep time:	Cook time:	Serving size:
1 (8-inch-round) loaf	15 minutes	45 minutes	1 ($^1/_2$-inch) slice

3 cups all-purpose flour	1 tsp. baking soda
$^2/_3$ cup currants	1 tsp. salt
3 TB. sugar	1 large egg
1 TB. caraway seeds	1 cup buttermilk
1 TB. baking powder	2 TB. unsalted butter, melted

1. Preheat the oven to 350°F. Line a baking sheet with parchment paper.

2. In a large bowl, stir together flour, currants, sugar, caraway seeds, baking powder, baking soda, and salt. Stir in egg and buttermilk until completely combined.

3. On a well-floured work surface and with well-floured hands, shape dough into a 5- or 6-inch ball and place on the baking sheet.

4. With a sharp knife, make two $^1/_2$-inch-deep slashes perpendicular to each other on top of loaf. Brush top with melted butter.

5. Bake for about 40 minutes or until loaf is a rich golden brown and a toothpick inserted into the center comes out clean.

6. Cool on the baking sheet for 10 minutes. Remove from the baking sheet and cool completely on a cooling rack. Cut into slices and serve warm or completely cooled.

BREAD HEAD

Because this soda bread contains a dried fruit such as currants or raisins, it's known as a "spotted dog" soda bread. It's also technically a "soda cake" because of the use of baking powder in the recipe.

Whole-Wheat Soda Bread with Toasted Oats

Whole wheat and toasted-oat nuttiness flavor this supremely easy bread. The tender texture comes from the addition of yogurt.

Yield:	Prep time:	Cook time:	Serving size:
1 (8-inch-round) loaf	20 minutes	40 minutes	1 (^{1}/$_2$-inch) slice

^{1}/$_3$ cup rolled oats

2 cups whole-wheat flour

1 cup all-purpose flour

3 TB. sugar

1 TB. baking powder

1 tsp. salt

^{3}/$_4$ tsp. baking soda

1 large egg

1^1/$_2$ cups plain yogurt

1. Preheat the oven to 350°F.

2. Spread oats onto a baking sheet and bake for about 5 to 10 minutes or until lightly toasted. Transfer toasted oats to a plate to cool completely.

3. Increase the oven temperature to 375°F. Line the baking sheet with parchment paper.

4. In a large bowl, stir together whole-wheat flour, all-purpose flour, sugar, baking powder, salt, baking soda, and cooled oats. Stir in egg and yogurt until completely combined.

5. On a well-floured work surface and with well-floured hands, shape dough into a 5- or 6-inch ball and place on the prepared baking sheet.

6. With a sharp knife, make two ^{1}/$_2$-inch-deep slashes perpendicular to each other in the top of loaf.

7. Bake for about 40 minutes or until loaf is a rich golden brown and a toothpick inserted into the center comes out clean.

8. Cool on the baking sheet for 10 minutes. Remove from the baking sheet and cool completely on a cooling rack. Cut into slices and serve warm or completely cooled.

BAKER'S DOZEN

A baking stone works great for baking free-form quick breads in place of a baking sheet. Keep the stone on a lower rack, and sprinkle it generously with cornmeal before placing the dough on top.

Orange-Raisin Scones

Fresh orange essence permeates every crumb of these amazingly tender craggy-crust scones.

Yield:	Prep time:	Cook time:	Serving size:
6 scones	15 minutes	30 minutes	1 scone

1½ cups all-purpose flour

3 TB. sugar

1½ tsp. baking powder

½ tsp. baking soda

½ tsp. salt

1 TB. orange zest

1 large egg yolk

½ cup plus 1 TB. buttermilk

3 TB. unsalted butter, very soft

⅓ cup raisins

1. Preheat the oven to 375°F. Place the oven rack in the center of the oven. Line a baking sheet with parchment paper.

2. In a large bowl, stir together flour, sugar, baking powder, baking soda, and salt. Stir in orange zest, egg yolk, buttermilk, softened butter, and raisins until combined.

3. On a well-floured work surface and with well-floured hands, shape dough into a disc about 5 or 6 inches in diameter. With a large knife or bench scraper, divide dough into 6 wedges. Evenly space wedges on the baking sheet.

4. Bake for about 30 minutes or until scones are firm and a light golden brown.

5. Cool on the baking sheet for 5 minutes. Remove from the baking sheet and cool completely on a cooling rack. Serve warm or completely cooled.

BAKER'S DOZEN

The secret to these scones isn't melting the butter, but ensuring the butter is very soft before you incorporate it into the dough. This keeps the scones from being too dense.

Sour Cream Biscuits

These tender, lightly sweetened biscuits get lots of flavor from the sour cream. A sprinkle of coarse sugar on top gives them a delectable crunch.

Yield:	Prep time:	Cook time:	Serving size:
6 biscuits	15 minutes	30 minutes	1 biscuit

1½ cups all-purpose flour	6 TB. unsalted butter, very soft
2 TB. sugar	1 large egg yolk
2¼ tsp. baking powder	3 TB. heavy cream
½ tsp. salt	3 TB. *turbinado sugar*
⅔ cup sour cream	

1. Preheat the oven to 375°F. Place an oven rack in the middle of the oven. Line a baking sheet with parchment paper.

2. In a large bowl, stir together flour, sugar, baking powder, and salt. Stir in sour cream, softened butter, and egg yolk until just combined.

3. On a well-floured work surface and with well-floured hands, pat dough into a rectangle about 1 inch thick. With a 2½-inch biscuit cutter or a drinking glass, stamp out biscuits and evenly space them on the baking sheet.

4. Brush each biscuit with heavy cream, and sprinkle turbinado sugar over top.

5. Bake for about 30 minutes or until biscuits are light golden brown and just firm.

6. Cool on the baking sheet for 5 minutes. Remove from the baking sheet and cool completely on a cooling rack. Serve warm or completely cooled.

LOAF LINGO

Turbinado sugar is made from sugar cane in a way that allows the sugar crystal to retain a bit of molasses. Its texture is coarser than granulated sugar, making it an ideal sugar topping when you want a bit of extra crunch. It's also known as *sugar in the raw* and *Demerara*. If you can't find any of these sugars, substitute granulated sugar.

Better Cheddar Biscuits

These biscuits are just like a soft and fluffy version of the crunchy and buttery cheddar goldfish-shape crackers.

Yield:	Prep time:	Cook time:	Serving size:
9 (2-inch) biscuits	15 minutes	20 minutes	1 biscuit

2 cups all-purpose flour

1 TB. plus 1 tsp. baking powder

$3/4$ tsp. salt

$1/2$ tsp. sugar

8 TB. unsalted butter, melted

$3/4$ cup buttermilk

$1^1/2$ cups sharp cheddar cheese, shredded

1. Preheat the oven to 375°F. Place the oven rack in the middle of the oven. Line a baking sheet with parchment paper.

2. In a large bowl, stir together flour, baking powder, salt, and sugar. Stir in 6 tablespoons melted butter, buttermilk, and cheddar cheese until combined.

3. On a lightly floured surface, roll dough into a 6×6-inch square about 1 inch thick. With a knife or bench scraper, cut dough into 9 (2-inch) biscuits and evenly space them on the baking sheet. Brush biscuits with remaining 2 tablespoons melted butter.

4. Bake for about 20 minutes or until biscuits are light golden brown and just firm.

5. Cool on the baking sheet for 5 minutes. Remove from the baking sheet, and cool completely on a cooling rack. Serve warm or completely cooled.

Make it your own: Add 1 minced garlic clove to the reserved 2 tablespoons melted butter to brush on biscuits before baking.

BREAD HEAD

Where did cheddar cheese originate? In the English village of Cheddar! The English love cheddar—it's the most popular cheese in the United Kingdom.

Sweet Potato Biscuits

These moist and delicate biscuits have a wonderful speckled orange hue and a slightly sweet and earthy taste.

Yield:	Prep time:	Cook time:	Serving size:
12 (2½-inch) biscuits	5 minutes, plus 45 minutes cool time for potato	75 minutes	1 biscuit

1 sweet potato or yam

1¾ cups all-purpose flour

4 tsp. firmly packed dark brown sugar

2¼ tsp. baking powder

½ tsp. baking soda

¾ tsp. salt

8 TB. unsalted butter, very soft

½ cup buttermilk

1. Preheat the oven to 425°F. Place the oven rack in the middle position. Line a baking sheet with parchment paper.

2. Prick sweet potato several times with a fork. Place potato on the baking sheet, and bake for 30 to 40 minutes or until potato is soft and can be easily poked with a sharp knife. Remove from the oven, and let potato cool completely, about 45 minutes.

3. Reline the baking sheet with another piece of parchment paper.

4. Discard cooled potato skin, and mash potato flesh with a fork. You should have about 1 cup mashed potato.

5. In a large bowl, stir together flour, brown sugar, baking powder, baking soda, and salt. Stir in mashed potato, butter, and buttermilk until just combined.

6. On a well-floured work surface, roll out dough to ¾ inch thick. With a 2¼-inch biscuit cutter, stamp out 12 biscuits and place on baking sheet.

7. Bake for about 25 minutes or until biscuits are golden brown and set.

8. Serve hot, or transfer biscuits to a cooling rack to cool completely.

Make it your own: You could add 1 teaspoon chopped fresh rosemary leaves or 1 tablespoon chopped fresh tarragon leaves to the dough in step 2 for herbed biscuits. Or pump up the heat by adding $1/8$ teaspoon cayenne. For a maple-flavored biscuit, substitute pure maple syrup for the dark brown sugar. To make this biscuit an extra-sweet treat, stir together 1 tablespoon sugar and $1/8$ teaspoon ground cinnamon and sprinkle over top of biscuits before baking. For a shortcake dessert, cut biscuits in $1/2$ and fill each with $1/3$ cup sweetened whipped cream and $1/3$ cup mixed berries.

BREAD HEAD

Did you know: the "yams" you see in the market are most likely just sweet potatoes. And sweet potatoes and yams aren't even related! Sweet potatoes are also classified as either firm or soft. In the United States, the softer variety is often labeled as a "yam" to distinguish between the two, even though it's not a true yam.

Super Easy Drop Biscuits

Rich with butter and cream, these biscuits are a snap to make!

Yield:	Prep time:	Cook time:	Serving size:
9 (2½-inch) biscuits	5 minutes	25 minutes	1 biscuit

2 cups all-purpose flour

1 TB. baking powder

2 tsp. sugar

¾ tsp. salt

½ cup plus 2 TB. light cream

½ cup whole milk

8 TB. unsalted butter, very soft

1. Preheat the oven to 375°F. Place the oven rack in the middle position. Line a baking sheet with parchment paper.

2. In a large bowl, stir together flour, baking powder, sugar, and salt. Stir in ½ cup cream, milk, and butter until just combined.

3. Using a medium retractable ice-cream scoop, drop 9 2½-inch mounds of batter onto the baking sheet. Brush tops of biscuits with remaining 2 tablespoons cream.

4. Bake for about 25 minutes or until biscuits are light golden brown around the edges.

5. Serve hot or transfer biscuits to a cooling rack to cool completely.

Make it your own: For whole-wheat drop biscuits, replace ½ cup all-purpose flour with whole-wheat flour. For herbed drop biscuits, add 4 teaspoons chopped dill. For a spicy drop biscuit, add 2 teaspoons coarsely ground black pepper.

BAKER'S DOZEN

If you don't have a retractable ice-cream scoop, you can use two soup spoons instead. Scoop the dough with one spoon, and use the other to release it onto the pan.

Toppings, Spreads, and Finishing Touches

Chapter

15

In This Chapter

- Prebake loaf washes
- Icing and glaze recipes for sweet finishing touches
- Sweet and savory complementary condiments

How you treat the top of your loaf before baking, and what you do to it after, have a big impact on its appearance and first impression.

This chapter is all about the finishing touches you can put on your no-knead artisan breads, as well as the fun accompaniments you can serve alongside. Of course flavor is important, but isn't it the yummy golden and shiny top on the loaf when it emerges fresh from the oven that first catches your eye? And what cinnamon bun would be complete without that gooey drizzle of sugary vanilla icing?

And although all the breads in this book are delicious on their own, I've included a few simple and easy-to-make spreads that will take your enjoyment of no-knead breads over the top. After you try a few of the flavored butters and cream cheese spreads, I hope they'll inspire you to conjure up your own flavorful concoctions!

And, when it comes to what you spread on your delicious homemade bread, don't limit yourself to supermarket-shelf butters. A plethora of premium and imported cultured butters are available and are meant to be savored. Bake a few loaves of bread, and have a butter-tasting party!

Essential Egg Wash

To give your breads a rich, golden look, brush this wash on the loaf before you bake it.

Yield:	Prep time:
2 tablespoons	1 minute

1 large egg   1 tsp. water

1. In a small bowl, whisk egg and water with a fork until egg is broken up and mixture is combined.

2. Use immediately, or cover tightly and store in the refrigerator for up to 4 days.

BAKER'S DOZEN

When applying the wash to your loaf, keep a light touch. If you slather on too much, the egg wash will drip down the sides of the loaf. If you're using a loaf pan, this could cause the bread to stick.

Cornstarch Baker's Glaze

This glaze is a baker's magic secret to achieving a clear, glasslike top on your loaves.

Yield:	Prep time:	Cook time:
1 cup	1 minute	2 minutes

2 tsp. cornstarch   1 cup water

1. Place cornstarch in a small saucepan and slowly whisk in water until smooth.

2. Heat over medium heat, stirring constantly, for 2 minutes or until mixture thickens and becomes translucent.

3. Remove from heat and let cool before using. Store in the refrigerator in an airtight container for up to 1 week.

DOUGH DON'T

When brushing this glaze on your loaf, avoid letting the glaze drip too far down the loaf and onto the bottom of the pan. This might inadvertently "glue" the loaf to the pan. If the loaf sticks to the pan, gently nudge and wiggle the bottom with a small knife or an offset spatula.

Vanilla Glaze

This sweet white glaze is the perfect finishing touch to breakfast breads like cinnamon rolls or coffee cake.

Yield:	Prep time:	Drying time:
about ⅓ cup	3 minutes	about 1 hour

1 cup confectioners' sugar

⅛ tsp. vanilla extract

3 tsp. milk

1. In a small bowl, stir together confectioners' sugar, milk, and vanilla extract until smooth.

2. Use immediately, or cover tightly and store in the refrigerator for up to 1 week. Stir before using.

Make it your own: Get creative and flavor this glaze to spice things up even more! Try adding a pinch of cinnamon, nutmeg, citrus zest, or even ⅛ teaspoon flavored liqueur.

BAKER'S DOZEN

You don't need to stock your kitchen with professional decorating tools to get that bakery-perfect drizzle. Simply fill a zipper-lock bag with icing, press the air out, and seal. When you're ready to decorate, snip a small piece off of a bottom corner and squeeze the bag to decorate.

Lemon Pucker Icing

This icing is as refreshing as a glass of super-tart lemonade on a summer day.

Yield:	Prep time:	Drying time:
about ⅓ cup	3 minutes	about 1 hour

1 cup confectioners' sugar   4 tsp. fresh lemon juice

1. In a small bowl, stir together confectioners' sugar and lemon juice until smooth.

2. Use immediately, or cover tightly and store in the refrigerator for up to 2 weeks. Stir before using.

BAKER'S DOZEN

This icing doesn't stay sticky for long and eventually dries to the touch. If you make it ahead of time, it's important to cover tightly so it doesn't dry out. If you make it more than a few hours ahead of time, store it in the refrigerator. Bring it to room temperature before using.

Sweet Whipped Cream

Lightly sweetened with just a hint of vanilla, this fluffy topping transforms sweet quick breads into the cream of the crop.

Yield:	Prep time:
1½ cups	5 minutes

1 cup heavy cream

2 tsp. sugar

½ tsp. vanilla extract

1. In a large bowl, whisk together cream, sugar, and vanilla extract until combined.

2. Continue to whisk vigorously for 3 or 4 minutes or until cream thickens. Use immediately or store in the refrigerator for up to 3 hours.

Make it your own: Add a pinch of cinnamon before whisking.

DOUGH DON'T

Once the cream begins to thicken, keep your eyes open and your whisking arm in control, or you might turn your whipped cream into butter! Soft peak stage (where the cream is the thickness of shaving cream) is ideal. After that, the cream will stiffen to stiff peak and, soon after, curdle.

Honey-Butter Spread

You'll want to spread this soft butter brimming with honey flavor on just about everything.

Yield:	Prep time:
about ²/₃ cup	3 minutes

¹/₂ cup (1 stick) unsalted butter, softened

2 TB. plus 2 tsp. honey

1. In a small bowl, stir together butter and honey until smooth.

2. Use immediately or store in the refrigerator for up to 2 weeks.

BAKER'S DOZEN

Sometimes you'll notice that your honey has crystallized and hardened during storage. You can bring it back to life by gently warming it in the jar in hot water until the honey returns to its liquid state. And for fuss-free measuring, lightly rubbing the measuring spoon or cup with vegetable oil or nonstick spray will prevent the honey from sticking.

Cream Cheese Spread

Creamy, slightly sweet, and with just the right amount of tang, this spread is the perfect alternative to butter for many of the richer breads in this book.

Yield:	Prep time:
about 1 cup	3 minutes

1 (8-oz.) pkg. cream cheese, softened

5 tsp. confectioners' sugar

$1/2$ tsp. vanilla extract

1. In a small bowl, stir together cream cheese, confectioners' sugar, and vanilla extract until smooth and fluffy.

2. Use immediately or store in the refrigerator for up to 1 week.

Make it your own: This spread is easy to customize. For a lemon cream cheese spread, swap out the vanilla extract for 1 tablespoon fresh lemon juice. For a crunchy alternative, stir in 2 tablespoons finely chopped nuts. If you're craving fruit, stir in 4 tablespoons any fruit preserve such as strawberry. For a savory spread that pairs perfectly with breads such as bagels, omit the sugar and vanilla extract, and stir in 4 tablespoons chopped red pepper. Or omit the sugar and vanilla extract, and stir in 4 tablespoons chopped dill, 4 teaspoons chopped onion, and 4 teaspoons chopped capers. For a cream cheese filling, to use on Danish or coffee cake, just stir in 1 tablespoon all-purpose flour.

BREAD HEAD

Created in 1872 in Chester, New York, tasty cream cheese has been hugely popular since A. L. Reynolds began distributing it in its hallmark foil wrapper as Philadelphia Brand Cream Cheese.

Double-Crumb Streusel

You can use these sweet and buttery crumbs to top any coffee cake.

Yield:	Prep time:
2¹/₂ cups	5 minutes

1 cup plus 2 TB. all-purpose flour

6 TB. firmly packed light brown sugar

1 TB. sugar

¹/₂ tsp. ground cinnamon

Pinch salt

8 TB. unsalted butter, melted

1. In a medium bowl, stir together flour, brown sugar, sugar, cinnamon, and salt.

2. Gently toss melted butter into flour mixture until just moistened.

3. Use immediately, or store in the refrigerator for up to 1 week.

DOUGH DON'T

Mix this streusel lightly. If overmixed, the tender texture can turn tough.

Rum Soaking Syrup

A healthy dose of rum in this syrup allows the flavor to come through in any pastry it's soaked with.

Yield:	Prep time:	Cook time:
2¹/₂ cups	2 minutes	1 minute

¹/₂ vanilla bean	1 cup water
1¹/₄ cups sugar	1 cup dark rum

1. Slice vanilla bean in ¹/₂ vertically and scrape out seeds.

2. Add bean to sugar and water in a small saucepan set over medium-high heat, and stir until sugar dissolves. Bring to a boil and remove from heat.

3. Stir in rum and let cool. Remove vanilla bean before using.

BREAD HEAD

A vanilla bean is the pod from the only known edible orchid. Because it's hand-pollinated, and because the pollination period is shorter than a day, vanilla is a very expensive flavoring, second only to saffron.

Quick Pizza Sauce

Loaded with tangy tomato flavor and fresh herbs, this sauce is a snap to prepare.

Yield:	Prep time:
about 1 cup	5 minutes

¾ cup canned crushed tomatoes, with juice

2 TB. tomato paste

1 TB. chopped fresh basil

2 tsp. sugar

1 tsp. chopped fresh oregano

Pinch salt

1. In a small bowl, stir together tomatoes with juice, tomato paste, basil, sugar, oregano, and salt until smooth.

2. Use immediately, or store in the refrigerator for up to 4 days.

Make it your own: For a chunky tomato sauce, replace crushed tomatoes with canned diced tomatoes and their juice.

BAKER'S DOZEN

Freeze it! You can make a large batch of sauce and freeze in cup portions so you can have a pizza topping at the ready.

Glossary

all-purpose flour   A general-purpose wheat flour suitable for a wide variety of baking and cooking.

arugula   A spicy-peppery garden plant with leaves that resemble a dandelion and have a distinctive—and very sharp—flavor.

autolyse   The rest period after mixing the ingredients together during which the gluten-forming proteins in the flour passively bond.

baguette   Also known as French bread, the name refers to the long, thin shape of loaf.

bake   To cook in a dry oven. Dry-heat cooking often results in a crisping of the exterior of the food being cooked. Moist-heat cooking, through methods such as steaming, poaching, etc., brings a much different, moist quality to the food.

balsamic vinegar   Vinegar produced primarily in Italy from a specific type of grape and aged in wood barrels. It's heavier, darker, and sweeter than most vinegars.

basil   A flavorful, almost sweet, resinous herb delicious with tomatoes and used in all kinds of Italian or Mediterranean-style dishes.

beer   A popular alcoholic drink made by the brewing and fermentation of cereal grain starches such as barley, wheat, corn, and rice.

bittersweet chocolate   A variety of chocolate that has an intense, mildly sweet chocolate flavor.

black pepper   A biting and pungent seasoning, freshly ground pepper is a must for many dishes and adds an extra level of flavor and taste.

blue corn meal   Made from ground whole blue corn, it has a sweet, earthy flavor and a pale, purple-blue color.

boule French for "ball," this refers to the round shape of a hearty, rustic French bread.

Brie A creamy cow's milk cheese from France with a soft, edible rind and a mild flavor.

brioche à tête A classic French enriched bread baked in a fluted mold and easily recognized by its round topknot.

buttermilk Originally, it was the liquid leftover after the churning of cream. Today, it's simply milk that's been fermented with bacteria.

cake flour A soft and fine high-starch, low-protein flour used primarily for cakes.

capers Salty briny buds of a Mediterranean plant, ranging in size from a *nonpareil* (about the size of a small pea), to larger and seedier grape-size caper berries produced in Spain.

caramelize To cook a food over low heat, usually in a small amount of fat, until the food softens and the sugars in the food darken and develop a sweet caramel flavor.

caraway A distinctive spicy seed used for bread, pork, cheese, and cabbage dishes.

cardamom An intense, sweet-smelling spice, common in Indian cooking and used in baking and coffee.

cheddar The ubiquitous hard cow's milk cheese with a rich buttery flavor that ranges from mellow to sharp. Originally produced in England, cheddar is now produced worldwide.

chèvre French for "goat milk cheese," chevre is a typically creamy-salty soft cheese delicious by itself or paired with fruits or chutney. Chèvres vary in style from mild and creamy to aged, firm, and flavorful.

chives A member of the onion family, chives grow in bunches of long leaves that resemble tall grass or the green tops of onions and offer a light onion flavor.

chop To cut into pieces, usually qualified by an adverb such as "*coarsely* chopped," or by a size measurement such as "chopped into $1/2$-inch pieces." "*Finely* chopped" is much closer to mince.

cider vinegar Vinegar produced from apple cider, popular in North America.

cilantro Very aromatic, cilantro is a member of the parsley family and used in Mexican cooking (especially salsa) and some Asian dishes. The seed of the cilantro is the spice coriander.

cinnamon   A sweet, rich, aromatic spice commonly used in baking or desserts. Cinnamon can also be used for delicious and interesting entrées.

clove   A sweet, strong, almost wintergreen-flavor spice used in baking and with meats such as ham.

cocoa   The unsweetened powder that results from removing the cocoa butter from finely ground cocoa beans.

confectioners' sugar   Granulated sugar that's been ground into a fine powder. It's used to make frostings, glazes, or sprinkled over pastries.

crumb   Refers to the texture of a baked item. For example, a cake may have a fine and tender crumb, and a bread may have an open, chewy crumb.

currant   A fruit often seen dried made from a small seedless grape and is similar to a raisin.

Dijon mustard   Pungent, spicy mustard made in the style of the Dijon region of France.

dill   A wispy, fresh-smelling herb perfect for eggs, salmon, cheese dishes, and of course, vegetables (pickles!).

dried cherries   Made from either tart or sweet cherries, dried cherries are moist, chewy, and great for snacking or adding to your favorite bread recipe.

drizzle   To lightly sprinkle drops of a liquid over food, often as the finishing touch to a dish.

durum   A very-high-protein wheat flour great for making pasta and bread.

Dutch oven   A heavy-duty pot (often ceramic coated) with a tight-fitting lid used for all types of cooking applications such as frying, braising, and baking.

ergot   A fungus that infects rye, the consumption of which results in ergotism, a condition that at the least causes convulsions and hallucinations.

extra-virgin olive oil   *See* olive oil.

flaxseed   Tiny crunchy seeds from the slender flax plant that are high in protein and omega-3 fatty acids.

flour   Grains ground into a meal. Wheat is perhaps the most common flour, but flour is also made from oats, rye, buckwheat, soybeans, etc. *See also* all-purpose flour; bread flour; cake flour; whole-wheat flour.

garlic A member of the onion family, a pungent and flavorful element in many savory dishes. A garlic bulb contains multiple cloves. Each clove, when chopped, provides about 1 teaspoon garlic. Most recipes call for cloves or chopped garlic by the teaspoon.

gluten Found in wheat flour, gluten is composed of the proteins gliadin and glutenin. When properly moistened, these proteins join to create stretchy strands that provide structure in bread.

ginger Available in fresh root, candied, or ground form, ginger adds a pungent, sweet, and spicy quality to a dish.

Gorgonzola A creamy and rich Italian blue cheese.

grate To shave into tiny pieces using a sharp rasp or grater.

hydration To combine with water. In relation to breads, it's the amount of water the flour has absorbed.

kalamata olives Traditionally from Greece, these medium-small long black olives have a smoky rich flavor. Look for unpitted olives.

knead To work dough to make it pliable so it holds gas bubbles as it bakes.

kosher salt A coarse-grained salt made without any additives or iodine.

lamination Alternating layers of butter and dough. This type of bread creates a particularly flaky and tender texture.

millet This crunchy seed is mildly sweet and can be cooked and eaten as a cereal or added to baked goods for texture. Lightly toasting before using increases the flavor.

mince To cut into very small pieces, about $^1/_8$-inch or smaller.

mise A French culinary term that means to have all your ingredients gathered and measured.

nutmeg A sweet, fragrant, musky spice used primarily in baking. Found either whole or ground, freshy grated nutmeg is especially flavorful.

offset spatula A sturdy metal spatula with a blade that bends at the point it meets the handle, allowing you to easily reach under foods. They come in a variety of sizes and are useful in tons of kitchen applications such as spreading batters and frosting cakes.

oil-cured olives These small wrinkly olives have been dry-cured and then re-plumped with oil. They have an intense flavor and should be used sparingly in dishes. For the easiest use in cooking, look for pitted olives.

olive oil A fragrant liquid produced by crushing or pressing olives. Extra-virgin olive oil—the most flavorful and highest quality—is produced from the first pressing of a batch of olives; oil is also produced from later pressings.

olives The fruit of the olive tree commonly grown on all sides of the Mediterranean. Black olives are also called ripe olives. Green olives are immature, although they're also widely eaten. *See also* kalamata olives and oil-cured olives.

oregano A fragrant, slightly astringent herb used in Greek, Spanish, and Italian dishes.

oven spring The final burst or expansion of a loaf of bread when it's subjected to the heat of the oven.

pancetta Similar to bacon, it's a dry, salt-cured meat made from pork belly.

Parmesan A hard, dry, flavorful cheese primarily used grated or shredded as a seasoning for Italian-style dishes.

pecans Rich, buttery nuts, native to North America, that have a high unsaturated fat content.

pepper jack cheese A spin-off of Monterey Jack cheese, it contains chopped hot peppers that make it tangy and zesty, with a moderate amount of heat.

pimento A small, sweet red pepper with a flavor similar to a red bell pepper. It's usually sold in jars, roasted, which gives it a smoky flavor.

pinch An unscientific measurement term, the amount of an ingredient—typically a dry, granular substance such as an herb or seasoning—you can hold between your finger and thumb.

pizza stone Preheated with the oven, a pizza stone cooks a crust to a delicious, crispy, pizza-parlor texture. It also holds heat well, so a pizza or other food removed from the oven on the stone will stay hot for as long as a half hour on the table.

poppy seeds Cultivated from the opium poppy plant, these tiny black seeds add a nutty crunch to foods, such as when sprinkled on breads or rolls before baking.

preheat To turn on an oven, broiler, or other cooking appliance in advance of cooking so the temperature will be at the desired level when the assembled dish is ready for cooking.

pumpernickel A type of hearty rye bread that's dark and slightly sweet.

queso fresco Translated in Spanish as "fresh cheese," this mild-flavored crumbly cheese is a common ingredient in Mexican cuisine.

reserve To hold a specified ingredient for another use later in the recipe.

ricotta A fresh Italian cheese smoother than cottage cheese with a slightly sweet flavor.

rolled oats Also known as old-fashioned oats, these oats are highly nutritious and filled with cholesterol-fighting fiber. They're made by passing steamed steel-cut oats through rollers to flatten them.

rosemary A pungent, woodsy herb used with chicken, pork, fish, and especially lamb. Use only the leaves from the tiny branchlike sprig. A little of it goes a long way.

sauté To pan-cook something in a small amount of fat such as butter or oil.

semolina The ground endosperm of milled durum wheat. If you can't find semolina flour, durum flour is a fine substitute.

shred To cut into many long, thin slices. Shredding can be performed on the large holes of a box grater.

slice To cut into thin pieces.

sour cream Cream that has been fermented and soured with lactic acid and bacteria.

sponge Also known as a yeast starter, poolish, or biga, this is an aged mixture of flour and water, sometimes with the addition of commercial yeast. It adds a wonderful tangy flavor when used in bread doughs.

sun-dried tomatoes Ripe tomatoes that have been placed in the sun to dry. They're highly concentrated in flavor and are available either dry or jarred, packed in water or oil.

sunflower seeds Harvested from the sunflower plant, the nutty kernels are a nutritious and flavorful addition to salads and baked goods. Look for unroasted and unsalted seeds.

tea bread   A sweetened bun, bread, or cake served with tea.

thyme   A minty, zesty herb often used to flavor meats, soups, and stews. Use only the small leaves from the sprig.

turbinado sugar   Sugar made from sugar cane in a way that allows the sugar crystal to retain a bit of molasses. Its texture is coarser than granulated sugar, making it an ideal sugar topping when you want a bit of extra crunch. It's also known as *sugar in the raw* and *Demerara*.

vinegar   An acidic liquid widely used as dressing and seasoning, often made from fermented grapes, apples, or rice. *See also* balsamic vinegar; cider vinegar.

wheat berries   The entire wheat kernel except for the hull. It comprises the bran, germ, and endosperm, making it extremely nutritious and an excellent source of fiber.

whole-wheat flour   Wheat flour that contains the entire grain.

yeast   Tiny fungi that, when mixed with water, sugar, flour, and heat, release carbon dioxide bubbles, which, in turn, cause the bread to rise.

yogurt   Milk that's been fermented by bacteria. The lactic acid produced gives yogurt its signature tang.

zest   The intensely aromatic and flavorful grated outer peel of a citrus fruit such as lemon, lime, or orange used for flavoring many foods both savory and sweet.

zester   A kitchen tool used to scrape zest off a fruit. A small grater also works well.

Resources

Here are some of my favorite books and resources, which can help you locate a wide assortment of baking information and supplies.

Books

Bread Baking: An Artisan's Perspective by Daniel T. DiMuzio.
Dig deeper into the science of bread-making in this informative textbook.

Six Thousand Years of Bread: Its Holy and Unholy History by H. E. Jacob.
Hungry for more history? Sink your teeth into this book that not only celebrates bread, but also gives detailed accounts of how bread has affected our lives throughout time.

Baking Equipment

Amazon
amazon.com
Find a wide array of general baking supplies here.

Breadtopia
breadtopia.com
Use this indispensable source to find bread bake ware, including baking stones, pizza peels, all shapes and sizes of proofing baskets, bench scrapers, bread knives, instant-read thermometers, mixing bowls, measuring cups and spoons, and bread storage boxes.

CHEFS
chefscatalog.com
CHEFS offers a huge selection of equipment such as Dutch ovens, cake pans, loaf pans, tube pans, baking sheets, and rolling pins.

King Arthur Flour

kingarthurflour.com

Log on here to find brioche pans, loaf pans, pizza pans, panettone papers, parchment sheets, Microplane graters, baking stones, and pizza peels.

Williams-Sonoma

williams-sonoma.com

Search this site for loaf pans, baking sheets, cooling racks, Silpat liners, pastry brushes, as well as a large selection of small kitchen gadgets.

Ingredients

Barry Farm Foods

barryfarm.com

Search here for flours, sweeteners, yeast, dried fruit, spices, pretzel salt, sea salt, barley malt syrup, and candied fruit.

Bob's Red Mill

bobsredmill.com

Find flours, organic flours, grains, a large assortment of oats, dried cherries, currants, shredded coconut, dry milk powder, nuts, and yeast.

King Arthur Flour

kingarthurflour.com

Turn here for a wide variety of flours and grains, yeast, cocoa, and almond paste.

Nuts Online

nutsonline.com

Look here for an endless variety of nuts and dried and candied fruits.

The Spice House

thespicehouse.com

Log in here for a great source for spices, salts, and vanilla extract.

Additional Resources

Baking911.com

baking911.com

Look here for information regarding everything baking, including terms, ingredients and how they interact, and common baking problems.

The Food Timeline

thefoodtimeline.com

This website offers historical information regarding everything food.

The Fresh Loaf

thefreshloaf.com

Log in here to find instructional videos, books, and links to baking blogs and baking websites.

YouTube

youtube.com

YouTube is unparalleled in the shear volume of instructional baking videos.

Measures

Converting measurements can sometimes seem intimidating. To help, I've included some common measurement equivalents. And for the times when you're short an ingredient for a recipe, I've included a few suggestions for substitutes. These tables don't just apply to the recipes in this book; you'll find them useful for many other cooking and baking recipes as well.

Measurement Equivalents

This ...	Equals This ...	Equals This ...	Equals This ...
1$\frac{1}{2}$ teaspoons	$\frac{1}{2}$ tablespoon	$\frac{1}{4}$ fluid ounce	
3 teaspoons	1 tablespoon	$\frac{1}{2}$ fluid ounce	
1 tablespoon	3 teaspoons	$\frac{1}{2}$ fluid ounce	
2 tablespoons	$\frac{1}{8}$ cup	1 fluid ounce	
4 tablespoons	$\frac{1}{4}$ cup	2 fluid ounces	
8 tablespoons	$\frac{1}{2}$ cup	4 fluid ounces	
12 tablespoons	$\frac{3}{4}$ cup	6 fluid ounces	
16 tablespoons	1 cup	8 fluid ounces	
1 cup	16 tablespoons	8 fluid ounces	
2 cups	1 pint	16 fluid ounces	
4 cups	2 pints	32 fluid ounces	1 quart
16 cups	4 quarts	128 fluid ounces	1 gallon

Temperature Conversions

To convert Fahrenheit to Celsius, subtract 32, divide by 9, and multiply by 5. To convert Celsius to Fahrenheit, divide by 5, multiply by 9, and add 32.

Fahrenheit	Celsius
32°F	0°C
50°F	10°C
100°F	37.8°C
120°F	48.9°C
150°F	65.6°C
200°F	93.3°C
212°F	100°C
240°F	115°C
250°F	121°C
270°F	132°C
300°F	149°C
320°F	160°C
350°F	177°C
400°F	205°C
450°F	233°C
500°F	260°C

Length Conversions

To convert inches into centimeters, multiply by 2.54.

U.S./Standard	Metric (Approximate)
1 inch	2.5 centimeters
6 inches	15.2 centimeters
8 inches	20.3 centimeters
9 inches	22.9 centimeters
12 inches (1 foot)	30.1 centimeters
13 inches	33.0 centimeters

U.S./Standard	Metric (Approximate)
2 feet	61.0 centimeters
3 feet (1 yard)	91.4 centimeters

Common Food Substitutions

If You're Out of This ...	Try This ...
Buttermilk, 1 cup	1 cup yogurt, 1 cup milk + 1 tablespoon lemon juice, 1 cup milk + 1 tablespoon vinegar, or 1 cup milk + 1 teaspoon cream of tartar
Egg, 1 large whole	2 yolks, 2 whites, or $3^1/_2$ tablespoons egg substitute
Egg white, large, 1	1 tablespoon powdered egg white or 2 tablespoons frozen egg whites
Egg yolk, large, 1	2 tablespoons powdered yolk or $3^1/_2$ teaspoons frozen yolk
Herbs, 1 tablespoon fresh	1 teaspoon dry
Honey, 1 cup	$1^1/_4$ cups white sugar, and increase recipe liquid by $^1/_4$ cup
Milk, 1 cup	$^1/_2$ cup evaporated milk + $^1/_2$ cup water or $^1/_4$ cup powdered milk + $^2/_3$ cup water

Index

C

E

F

I

CHECK OUT THESE BEST-SELLERS

More than 450 titles available at booksellers and online retailers everywhere!

978-1-59257-115-4

978-1-59257-900-6

978-1-59257-855-9

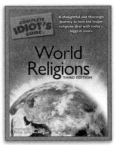

978-1-59257-222-9

978-1-59257-957-0

978-1-59257-785-9

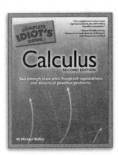

978-1-59257-471-1

978-1-59257-483-4

978-1-59257-883-2

978-1-59257-966-2

978-1-59257-908-2

978-1-59257-786-6

978-1-59257-954-9

978-1-59257-437-7

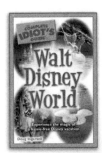

978-1-59257-888-7

ALPHA   idiotsguides.com